To Celeste,
Happier Ever After —
Brenda

LIFE HAS NO EXPIRATION DATE

Misadventures of a Single Senior

BRENDA FRANK

D0873679

with

R. H. KIRSHEN

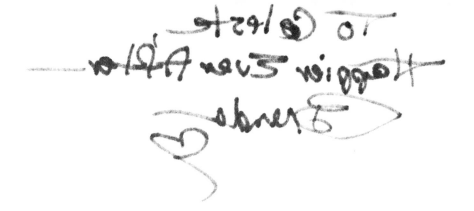

Published in the United States by
Sugar Grove Press
Pompano Beach, Florida 33062
http://www.sugargrovepress.com

Life Has No Expiration Date / Misadventures of a Single Senior
By Brenda Frank
Virtual Collaborator r.h. kirshen
Cover Design by Alfred Frohman
Back cover photo by Bette Marshall

Paperback ISBN: 978-1-7368447-3-1

Dedication

For Judy Levy Fryer
To most selfless woman I've ever known.

To Anagha,
I am so happy you are in my life.
Your kindness and generosity speak volumes about who you are.
Wishing you and yours a long and healthy life filled with joy.
Namaste

To you, my readers,
May you go through life benefiting from whatever comes your way.
Wishing you happily ever after.
Brenda

Contents

Preface

"We have enough money for you to retire." *Wait, was that a question or a statement?* I can't remember the many times FLOML[1] brought up wanting me to fold up my tent and follow him into the sunset. I was still selling real estate and earning money that we had no problem spending.

His was a love-hate situation. He loved the money, but hated, or resented the fact that I still worked. After almost fifty-six years, he calculated we had enough money. Some of our retirement income was now augmented by an inheritance from my parents, not mega dollars, but sound investments, and some cash, which allowed us to supplement our income and provided us the added luxury of having the financial freedom to retire.

"Retire to what," I asked?

"To do whatever we want."

By this time, we had nothing in common. He played golf, sailed a custom-made boat in Biscayne Bay, or spent weeks at our home, alone, in Costa Rica. Okay, alone??? Whatever…

I worked and was on call seven days a week. On the weekends, I enjoyed our condo in South Beach. I looked forward to the twice-monthly Lincoln Road Antique Shows, an occasional movie at the foreign picture theatre, museums, concerts, and dinners out. Sometimes as a couple, sometimes on my own.

With money coming in it's easy to lull yourself into thinking that somehow it will always be there. He considered starting to use our retirement money to live on. "We have plenty," he cried.

"What if one of us gets sick and would need to spend big bucks for treatment?"

His retort made my blood run cold. "You can't. We won't have enough." Then coldly staring directly in my face, he said in a cold monotone voice, "Then you'll die."

I think his message was more about me than for himself because when he needed quadruple by-pass surgery, he did not ask how much anything was costing to keep HIM alive!

"What about traveling?" I inquired. Ever since I was a young woman, I looked forward to saving enough money so one day, I could travel the world, with or without him.

"You can't."

Wow! When can I start being retired??? I can hardly wait. Let's see, hmmm, I can take walks, watch TV, go to the movies together, only if it's something that interests him, but not too many live shows, they cost big bucks. New clothes? Why? I wasn't going anywhere!

Since being on my own and having to work for two more years after he left to reconsolidate some retirement money that I had to give him, as well as having to sign over the Miami Beach condo, the Costa Rica property, his boat, and most of my retirement fund ... like Smokey, he made out like a bandit. As Zsa Zsa Gabor once put it so eloquently, "You never really know a man until you divorce him."

I am by far not rich, but I am not poor, at least not yet. I invested in conservative annuities. What I am rich in, is peace of mind. Being independent brings about less stress and more freedom.

The following stories could not have happened if I did not have the freedom of choice. Regardless of what you want to do, don't wait. Break through your gate before it's too late!

---

1. Former Love of my Life

The New You

PART I

ONE

The New You

H i there. Remember me? If you read, *Divorced After 56 Years, Why Am I Sooo Happy?* then we have already met. If not, this sequel will assure you that I am still Sooo Very Happy.

What makes me happy is doing, what I want, when I want, and with whomever I want. I keep my expectations in line with my abilities and what is achievable. I do not set unattainable goals. By that, I mean I have never been snowboarding in my younger days, and I am not about to challenge my bone density by starting now.

The same could be said for joining Cirque du Soleil. Get over it; that's reaching for the unattainable. Reaching too far out can land you flat on your face, a place you do not want to be.

Think practical, and be comfortable, at least when you first test the water. As Stacey Charter, a world-famous online quotidian once said, "Life is all about timing...the unreachable becomes reachable, the unavailable becomes available, the unattainable...attainable. Have the patience, wait it out. It's all about timing."

Regardless of how or why, you are now single. Your statistical count goes from being a twosome to a one-some. You are by yourself. Just don't call yourself a-lone-some. One thing's for certain, your life will change, and it's up to you to make it better. You are now a committee of one. Your voting tallies will be unanimous.

Ask yourself, "What do I want to do with the rest of my life?" For starters, how about reaching into your mental attic and dusting off all your stored fantasies.

Cross the Atlantic on the Queen Mary? Get thee to a Casbah or see the pyramids along the Nile? Whatever, they are yours, you own them, lock, stock, and barrel. Use them or lose them.

Do you have a plan? No? Make one. It's time to move on. I know folks who make lists of to-do things that are so long they become overwhelmed and wind up doing nothing but sittin' and sighin'. Put as many items as possible on your list that are realistic for you; this is your list. Let's say four.

That's enough…for now.

Wait a minute… that voice in your head is talking to you. It's telling you something, whether you want to pay attention to it or not. Try as we might, we cannot, like our cell phone at the movies, shut off our thoughts.

Step one: Stop and listen to your inner voice. Perhaps it is churning out suggestions.

Step two: Start doing. Begin with something small. It may be, *I should go for a walk this afternoon.* Then do it. Practice makes purrfect.

Step three: Complete one thing, cross it off your list, and add another, but never let that list overload your brain.

Think about it. What, or who can get in the way of accomplishing your goals? More than likely the answer is *you*. Have a meeting with yourself. Look in the mirror and ask, why?"

Stop listening to your friends. As much as you love one another, they don't know the new you. How can they, when you don't know the new you!"

TWO

You're Fired! No, I Quit!

A fter fifty-six years of marital bliss and some marital miss, we were no longer as compatible as we (thought) we were when we were married at ages eighteen and nineteen. I was shocked... yeah, right! What I came to realize was that I didn't find out what real happiness was until I got married...and then it was too late.

Analyzing my situation and speaking with other men and women, I have determined marriage can be compared to a business deal. When you invest, one of the first things you look for is appreciation...unless of course, you just bought a new car. There are investments you make, that over the years lose their value; even that *must have* piece of jewelry you fell in love with, and years later wonder what it was that you were attracted to.

Add that to the growing pile of *WWIT's* -*What was I thinking?* When you try to dispose, re-gift or sell it. You'll discover it may have lost most of its value, and most of its luster.

Four things can happen in a relationship; it gets better or worse, stays the same or submissiveness sets in. In my situation, things got bad, got better, stayed the same and then lost their value.

Call it divorce, discharged, or dismissed. As I see it now, after fifty-six years I was fired. In retrospect I should have quit.

My designation was that of *the wife*. My job description was to cook, clean, shop, be a lover, and sometimes travel companion. Many businesses have periodic evaluations of their workers to consider if they are deserving of a raise, more vacations, or just the assurance of not losing their jobs. I think Caryl Rivers put it best when she said:

> Men have jobs, while women have Roles: Mother, Wife, Goddess, Temptress, etc. That's probably why it's so hard for women to rewrite the rules. You're not just changing a job description, but an ancient myth. You're revising the Bible, Poetry, Legend and Psychoanalytic Scripture.

Hourly or weekly wage increases? That's a joke. I paid my way. No one supported me. I worked for free and on our twentieth anniversary, discovered our contract had been adulterated by my boss's i.e., husband's, adultery.

Along with my presumed responsibilities I was a full-time mother to two boys while selling real estate, another 24/7 job. It was a balancing act and there were times I opted for losing a sale rather than running the risk of losing the job that I thought was for life; you know, that whole "til death do us part" detail of my marriage.

When I was summarily fired, I learned I had not protected myself financially and there was no severance pay. I was dismissed with some of my sweat equity but not all of it. My 'boss' cleaned out the *till* before he cleaned out his closet.

"A woman's work is never done." No truer words have ever been spoken or written.

Hopefully my narrative may only resonate for couples who were born before 1965. Today's women are a lot more independent and smarter. One of the twosome, usually the man, has the option of retiring from his job; often with a lifetime pension while his wife has a lifetime sentence.

He no longer must show up at a particular place at a predetermined time and work a certain number of hours that he may or may not enjoy for someone he may or may not like. His chains have been severed.

But his significant other doesn't have the luxury of retiring. Regardless of her age, her job description remains the same. Cook, clean, shop and do whatever household chores that were pre-determined decades before. If she dares to defy her workload, she could be swept away like this morning's toast crumbs.

My advice to all newcomers who agree to the terms of the position of wife; take the job but get a guarantee of severance pay and retirement benefits in writing. Renew your commitment, perhaps every five to ten years...that is if you haven't already been fired or said, "I quit."

THREE

Status Change

On July 15, 2015, like switching political party affiliations from Democrat to Republican, my status changed. That was the day I became a new statistic. My status, married, became, status, divorced. I changed ranks. I became the general of my domain.

Regardless of how or why you are single, your household now numbers one. I am a happy party of one and a committee of one where my vote and decision is permanently unanimous. Try it, you'll like it!

When my flight of fifty- six years crash-landed, I picked myself up and began flying solo, soaring high, and loving it. Don't be afraid to get on your launching pad and get ready for the flight of your life. One of the many perks of living on your own is finding what you subconsciously may have been seeking for many years; yourself. During my marriage I worked on being the person I thought he wanted me to be, while suppressing the person I wanted to be...the real me.

Along with other women of my generation, which was at the beginning of the Freidan/Steinem women's lib movement, it became a necessity for us to learn to juggle housework and family while also contributing to the family coffers.

What that meant was that I went to the supermarket **after** work. Before Women's Lib, a *stay-at-home* (that term didn't exist then), wife and mother, meant you could grocery shop during the day and make dinner before everyone got irritable and hungry.

Now, they're waiting for you to come home, like baby birds in the nests with their beaks up tweeting to be fed. In *those* days we didn't have the luxury and convenience of todays' drive-through fast food or pre-made take out dinners.

Regardless that the times *they were 'a-changin'*; when decision time on major matters came up, I was denied full partnership.

"Surprise!" FLOML cried ecstatically one evening. "How do you like my new Corvette?"

Change and adaptation evolve slowly. Once I was on my own, I started peeling away years, like layers of wallpaper, and lo and behold; "Well, hello! Where have YOU been all my life?"

I regained my confidence which was waiting in the wings, and my sense of humor returned. It had been such a slow gradual loss over so many years that I wasn't aware it was missing. It had eroded, like the beaches through climate change. Today, to paraphrase a Billy Joel song, *I Love Me Just the Way I Am.*

There is an expression that declares, *two can live as cheaply as one.* This is true if you believe W.A. Criswell, when he said, "Two can live as cheaply as one…if one doesn't eat and the other goes naked."

Whoever coined that phrase, but obviously did not run home from school brandishing any math trophies. My grocery bill was reduced considerably and eating out and paying for one, well…you do the math. Clothing costs, half, phone bills… no need to go on, you get the message. Although the cost of becoming one was extravagant, I learned you do get what you pay for.

While we are young, what we desire and ultimately own defines us. This is especially visible to outsiders who think they know who we are and judge us by our possessions.

One day you wake up and decide you've had enough. Then you start getting rid of all your must-haves, knickknacks, your *good* China and silver, and in at least half of all marriages in the U.S., wives and husbands.

Lost and found? When I was young, I had a lean and slim figure, which evolved into a slim-ish mature one. Trying to maintain or lose weight is a losing battle, but unfortunately not lost from my hips. I gain pounds and lose ounces. The two pounds I gain in one day takes two weeks to lose eight ounces. Two challenges, age and gravity, work against you.

Bear in mind, after a certain age, whatever that age is, your body begins to lose its resiliency and elasticity. Losing too much weight can make you look old and wrinkly, like dried out crepe paper from last night's sudden rainstorm. Stay the way you are unless you are morbidly obese. Then seek medical help.

The word premature no longer applies to me. I am past the age of going prematurely grey and I am too old to die young. When I need assistance that requires reaching out to someone on the internet and speaking to a 'team member' with a faceless voice who asks what my name is and may she or he call me by my first name, I answer "Yes." She or he replies, "Awesome." "Hmmm, I wonder, do they mean my name or that I remembered it?"

You know you are getting older, and hopefully wiser, when your footwear of choice are sneakers, and you don't obsess that the red stripes on your blouses don't exactly match the red in your comfy pull-on stretch pants. Women, and especially men, before stepping out in public, check that zipper!

Let's eliminate counting age by the numbers. Why not classify age by sectors. I am in the sixty-five to eighty-year-old sector, although sometimes I feel like forty -five. Conversely though, there are times when I feel my age, oops, I mean the far end of my sector. Regardless, don't make long-term plans, it's time to live in the moment. Do it now!

FOUR

Get Thee out of the Gray Zone

A t 7 a.m., as the sun was rising above the horizon, I joined a group of women who were having a mindfulness session on the beach. "Go for the colors. Pick a color, any color, and be mindful of it all day" enthused the leader. Regardless that the sand was the color of oatmeal, and I was sitting on a lavender blanket under a blue sky sprinkled with bright white marshmallow clouds, I chose red, after explaining to one of my more depressed companions that "dull gray" is not a color.

By being mindful of that color, everything suddenly became brighter. I felt like Dorothy as she stepped out of her black and white celluloid world into the technicolor land of Oz.

Gray thoughts take over slowly. Some organically, some intrinsically, and then one day, "Hello, is that YOU?" You take a long hard look into the unforgiving mirror that gives us the truth, the whole truth, and nothing but the truth. Silently, you talk to the mirror; "Mirror, mirror on the wall, am I still the fairest of them all?' In an awkward horror-stricken moment, the mirror refuses to answer on the grounds it will be blamed for the loss of the youthful blush on our faces and the once present shine of our hair growing dim; no longer full and lustrous.

Sir and/or madam, wake up and smell the hair dye, it's time to wash that gray, not only out of your hair, but out of your life. Although aging is inevitable, and we recognize that the spring in our step needs oiling and possibly even a replacement, where is it written that we must give in to being an oldster who rests and rusts? I'd rather rock n' roll.

Are you becoming one of those tedious men and women we used to run away from, who complain, are judgmental, and are wearisome to be around? Those are the people I refer to as the *Graybeards*. They are stuck in that sooty, mushy, gray zone.

The options are to get up and get out. Mix it up. Do things that involve people younger than yourself. That means everyone, including toddlers, who love to be read to. Volunteer in pre-school programs and work yourself up to the high schoolers. At that point you may become the student in programs where teenagers are teaching the seniors.

These young men and women help where the seniors seem to need it most, with their computers and electronic devices, or anything that comes with more than one paragraph of instructions. They enjoy teaching, especially if their senior-students are eager to learn.

Attend events that interest you. "Meet-Up" groups are a great resource for varying activities, and there are hundreds of them involving a myriad of interesting and educational topics. You'll meet people you have things in common with, who would shudder if they knew you might have just dusted yourself off after escaping from the gray zone. You may want to keep that a secret and promise yourself never to enter there again.

Don't lose your enthusiasm and for god's sake don't lose your sense of humor, assuming you had one to lose! If you didn't, we won't send you back to that gray dust pile if you do what comes naturally, smile!

Get excited, plan something fun, a party, a cruise, a vacation. Anticipation and the excitement that goes with it could become the best part of your life. By denying yourself things, you deny life. I'd rather live a shorter time and be happy than a longer time being miserable.

If I can't get up, get out, and do things and have a good time then, "Check please, I'm outta here." It's easier to give in than to get up. As one ages that *get up and go* loses steam. No one is sure where it goes, but your mind is stronger than your body. Think it and your body will follow. Your body has no choice but to go along for the ride.

Everyone is moving along on this conveyor belt of life so there can be room for the newbies. This writer, too old to die young, wants to kick the bucket with a list that is all checked off. Until that happens, make every day a red-letter day!

FIVE

Aging for Dummies

A ging is not for the faint of heart. It takes a lifetime to get it right.

Assuming you don't fall out of your crib, get run over on your way to school, or fail to survive an overturned school bus, you'll wake up one day old and gray.

When you do awaken, but still occupy that nether region between sleep and consciousness, your mother or father will be uttering something directly at you, and you will hear yourself repeating those same words that made you grimace every time you heard one of them voicing the same thought, or in today's lingo you will realize, *OMG, I've become my parents.*

Whether you call it reincarnation or just plain ghosts, they are with you. If you're a woman, it's your mother. If you are the man in the family, you stare in horror as your father shows up one morning in your bathroom mirror.

"Howdy stranger, how did you get in *here?*" You are then reminded of Rogers and Hammerstein, who wrote *June is busting out all over.* Those hairs, like weeds in a beautiful garden, are suddenly bursting forth from your ears, nose, and your chinny chin chin. More important though than the hairs themselves, is the nagging question...*when did this happen?*

You made it. You graduated from daycare, pre-kindergarten, kindergarten, and your pre-college years. From scratched knees to bruised egos, you finally arrived on a college campus. You passed through the revolving doors and experiment, discover, and bloom; emerging on the other side as an independent adult and hopefully wiser for that costly, *it will take me HOW LONG to pay off my student loans?* opportunity.

Now that you've gotten this far, where do you go from here? Anywhere you want! You have reached the base camp of the mountain range called life.

Along your journey, you'll struggle with career choices, anticipations, and frustrations. You will experience disappointment, acceptance, rejection, and resignations, in dealing with what is, what was, and all those, 'I quit'.

The fun part will be falling in love with your best friend. Marrying, or committing to be a lifetime partner, and having children who are miniature images of yourself, will allow you to raise these little people to be the people you always wanted to be.

Whoever said we only go around once never held an offshoot of themselves. And so, my dear friends this is the circle of life...succinctly and simply put. This is the summation to the story of aging as I see it. Now, it's up to you to fill in the blanks.

SIX

Diary of an Ex-Housewife

S hould I start with, 'Dear Diary'? Or is that just a time and paper waster? Daily chores out of the way. Shopped for necessities. Did a little (very little) 'straightening up' in my condo.

I ate more than necessary to keep me fueled and now I am ready to write; except for one thing. It's sooo quiet.

When I have more things to do than there are hours in the day, I chomp at the bit to write while I run around finishing chores. My head is like a washing machine crammed full of clothes bubbling over with what I want to say, excited to start writing.

Now what? Too quiet. Not enough tension to keep my batteries charged for the task of writing. Waaait a minute! What is that rumbling noise? It sounds like a hungry bear. Gotta check it out.

Mystery solved. The drainpipe under my new sink is vibrating. Running water relieves the noise; must find out why. First thing tomorrow I'll call the plumber.

Well, that seems to be enough stress to get me started. "Gentlemen", or in this case, "Lady, start your engine!" I am fired up, having run out of excuses.

I can now proceed with making new memories. Let's open the ol' diary and put in another installment, transferring my thoughts, like spooning cookie dough onto parchment paper.

I have reached a ripe old age where not everyone makes it this far. If they have, they're replacing body parts. When I go through TSA security, I'm able to skip the full-body scan being that I am over seventy-five but not before being asked if I have any metal in me. As of this writing, I answer, smugly, "Not yet."

When I had a big birthday looming, I decided it's never too early to start celebrating. For my pre-birthday present, I gave myself the right to not eat anything I don't want. I'd be retreating into my childhood when eating was not a pleasure. Although now I do like many of the foods I didn't when I was a small child, like sour cream and fried liver...no, not together!

Today's must-eat foods include avocado. I'm not a big fan, after making the effort, even though "They're so good for you!" I never heard anyone say "Boy, I can't wait to sink my teeth into a ripe avocado, so I'm not so sure people *really* do like them.

My interest does get peaked though when avocados are smashed and smashed into guacamole. Adios yogurt. Can't call me a vegetarian, but it's only on very rare occasions I crave a hot dog or rib steak, and although I enjoy swimming with them, I hardly eat fish either. I don't want them hooked and cooked for me.

My plan is to die healthy while not fitting into any category food-wise. I am not a bona fide vegetarian, though thoughts of live animals being slaughtered are enough to usually assuage my appetite for meat or chicken. No vegan, and definitely not keto which, I have been told, causes among other issues, bad breath, fatigue, vomiting, and confusion. I can get that on my own.

I drink whole cows' milk, enjoy a stack of pancakes soaked in real maple syrup, and relish fried eggs slithering around in the butter. Sticks, cups, sandwiches, and half-gallon tubs, like having too much money, one cannot have too much ice cream. Can this be for real, or is *Prevention Magazine* just messing with me? Regardless, my freezer is crammed full of ice cream, my dinner of choice.

SEVEN

Happy Days

_I_t has been written, the two happiest days in a man's life are the day he buys a boat and the day he sells it. Note the key word in that sentence is _man_.

Now, what about us women? I can't say for certain if Sept. 7, 1958, my wedding day, was the happiest day of my life. But what I can declare with certainty is that July 15, 2015, the day my divorce became final, if not the happiest day, certainly ranks close to the top of the chart.

Some of the events that are on par with that date are having my two sons, buying our first home, and reaching the point where we had more money than days of the week left over.

Placing close, but not quite being relegated to the upper tier was getting my real estate license, and seeing the real Camino Real in Mexico, after struggling for years in high school learning to read and write Spanish from a textbook entitled *The Camino Real.*

Marriage was not all bad. Taking advantage of an American Express special offer, who can forget the thrill of flying to Paris on the supersonic passenger airliner Concorde for our thirtieth wedding anniversary?

What is happiness? It can run the gamut from being relaxed to being secure, to being on cloud nine, and anything in between that might raise your spirits. When you look in the mirror you see it on your face.

A certain luminosity takes over that seems to be out of your control, but a good out-of-control. Or that look of being excited by something that happened that you didn't expect, like your scale showing, yes indeedy, today you have achieved your desired weight or winning the lottery. Happy could even be your sister-in-law canceling your lunch date or finding out you don't need a root canal. Truthfully, though, the key to happiness is the willingness to enjoy every moment of your life.

The list is endless, and everyone's happy place is not, well … everyone's happy place. You have your own. Happiness is personal, and whatever brings a spring to your step and makes you feel lighthearted, and even lightheaded, is your kind of happy. Don't accept someone else's happiness; like their old shoe, it won't fit. It's up to you, a party of one, to make your own happiness.

EIGHT

Four Stages of Life

T here are four stages of life:

- When you are born, you are who you are
- When you become what others want you to be
- When you become what you want to be
- When you become what you have become

When you are born, you are who you are

Waah! with a cry or a yelp, someone will be there to answer the call to feed, coddle, and protect you. One of the first things a baby learns is how to get attention. I'm hungry, I need a diaper change, I have a pain, I need company, he's not my father. These are the things that occupy a baby's new-formed brain. Need, desire, want. Babies learn fast and those who care for them learn too. Call it manipulation or train the brain. The formative years set you on the path from *who you are* to what you will become.

When you become what others want you to be

You have ideas, beliefs, and thoughts about things that matter and then second guess yourself. You are anxious about what your parents, teachers, friends, and your SO (Significant Other) think about you and may disparage your opinion on any number of topics. Then the other person's vocal influence takes over your thoughts.

Do you anticipate criticism, as in, 'waiting for the other shoe to drop?' Do you feel the need to restrain what you can or cannot say or do?

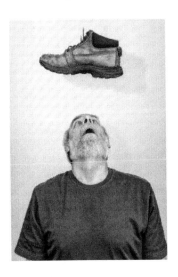

I was warned against, 'talking shop,' which in my case was real estate. Many social dialogues turn to the stock market, bragging about the gains and forgetting the losses; sorta like a day at the races, which restaurants are the newest and best, and the aforementioned real estate. When the subject arose, oft times the exchange was addressed to me, being that I was a licensed full-time realtor. In many of those cases "SO" would re-direct the conversation to himself. I was relieved since it took the pressure off me to have to mind what I said, to whom I said it, and why I said it.

In my situation SO had a remarkable memory. If I said something he felt was inappropriate, every six weeks; you could set your calendar to it, he would have a diatribe and regurgitate my remarks and tell me how someone's eyes rolled at something I said and why did I say it? Then the inquisition would start, and I would have to defend myself to him. *Hey, someone call me a lawyer!*

Archie Bunker, grimacing through clenched teeth would tell Edith on the hit series of the '70s *All in the Family,* "Stifle yourself Edith" whenever she voiced an opinion of her own that he didn't agree with. I was Edith. *When you become what others want you to be,* it is time to consider making the move into the next stage of your life.

When you become what you want to be

Well, here I am, marooned, on an island made for one. The ship sailed away. On one hand, with a sense of relief, but on the other, who am I, if I am alone?

Workwise, I am one person, confident in my skills and compassion, and believe in my work as a realtor. Socially, not so much. I felt like a polar bear on a severed iceberg drifting towards the unknown.

Regardless of my self-confidence at work, how would I make it socially? What could I possibly offer that anyone would want to hear other than real estate updates?

After fifty-six years of being a twosome, would I be welcomed as a onesome? Most of my friends were married couples. Would I still be included in their social gatherings? And even if I was, how could I hold up my end of a conversation? Would I even know how to begin one?

I was shot down for expressing opinions that might not have coincided with you-know-who's. Socially speaking it was all I knew. My insecure thoughts left me with a lack of confidence and minimal social skills as a single woman.

Oh well, let's dip those feet in the frigid water and see if I could make it back to the *mother berg.*

And I did. I eased into my new role, at first with trepidation, but quickly adapted to my new place in society. I sensed a sigh of relief while my role was being defined. I made it clear that when I was invited to join married couples, that any expenses, such as at dinner, gift-giving, or sharing cabs, I would always pay my fair share.

A widow, at first gets lots of sympathies. Use this adjustment time to reposition yourself as an independent person who may not need, as much as want, companionship.

As a message to others who are afraid to try going it alone, this is not your (grand)mother's generation. Get out there! The internet is waiting with open arms to introduce you to clubs, organizations, social gatherings. Make new friends. That way you are making it solely on your own with no dark shadows hovering about to remind you of days past. This is your time to *become what you want to be.*

When you become what you have come to be

One day, when you least expect it, you'll wake up with a smile on your face looking forward to a day that is stress-free regarding not having to satisfy another. Breakfast, whenever, or maybe never? Who cares? Health reports be damned. Besides, almost every day the *mavens* change, keeping us clamoring to buy this, no, eat that, do this, no, not so much, do that. I have a headache? Oh yes, there are at least five remedies for it!

It is now your time to do what you want, when you want, with or without whomever you may or may not want to be with. Oh, what a relief it is!

You look in the mirror and see you! Not the new you, but the one who was maturing and waiting in the wings to step out on the world stage to present yourself, confidently, as who you now are. You have reached your destination. You have *become what you have come to be.*

NINE

Memoirs of a Newly Single Person

Besides having to figure out how bills are paid and to whom, another whelming task I needed to tackle in the first days of being on my own was the computer. In the frontier days every time I passed by, it gave off a sardonic smirk of knowing more than me and wise to the fact; "You'll never get it."

Everything was good in the olden days, Before Computers (BC). Then came the dawning of Aquarius, oops, I mean of computers. They came in one size: big, and bulky. Behind it was countless tangled cables and, on the floor below was a box of paper that threaded into the computer. My thoughts, more often than I could count was, *Should I or shouldn't I?* Naah, too much stuff to throw over the balcony and declare it an accident.

We rocket to outer space; we live in inner space. Where the hell is cyberspace? It's not a ride in Disney World, and upon Googling it, you confirm that it's not a theme park.

Cyberspace is a place to send your mind, the way you send your children to summer camp. What you think, and your typed thoughts are all that is necessary to become a member in good standing of this magical, mystical place.

I run out of excuses and must stop finding important chores to do, like dusting the light bulb in my bedside lamp or condensing my bras and panties together in the same drawer. Upon completing this task, I conclude they were all happier in their own space, so I put them back where I found them.

I needed to learn how to navigate this unknown, foreboding, mysterious pathway that, when successful, gives you a lightness and satisfaction of mind and body. This accomplishment can only be reached by creating and, most importantly, remembering your own personal and secret code.

Foreboding, and anticipating the worst, I turn on my computer. Taking a deep breath, I press 'return'. Eureka!

I am 'in'. I get up, do a little dance, sit down again, and start working.

The first step is setting up my own confidential and personal code. Choose a password. That's easy. Pick a name or number.

The second requirement, a username, takes more of your attention and concentration. That, for your eyes-only code, must include at least eight letters, one upper case letter, a number, and a symbol. Where was I when the pound# sign was replaced by hashtag#? Whenever I see one, I still think first of tic-tac-toe. And hashtag? Didn't I have those incised a while back by a dermatologist?

Memo to self: Don't even think you will remember either of those codes, never mind both of them, which is the necessary key to enter the inner sanctum of the netherworld of infinite information.

I must write them down, and soon. Where should I keep them? Hmm, Did I use a capital letter or stick in a number? Did I use Jeff's birthdate or Kevin's? Did I use B1398000000F (my initials wrapped around the present population of China? Oh well, it will come to me. Yea, right. Like that's gonna happen!

I am sitting at my computer, disheveled, wearing an old holey cotton tee-shirt and a pair of cutoff jeans, sipping red wine from a coffee cup.

It's 9:30 a.m. A neighbor does a 'pop in'. Who cares if she's dismayed at what's in my old cup imprinted with, I♥Bagel Nosh? She should've called first. I am happy about the interruption and the delay of the inevitable. We chit-chat.

The bad hostess I am, by not offering her a cup of wine or even a glass of water, she gets the hint and finally leaves. Facing the reality of what I need to do, I tell myself, be positive because this site will be user-friendly.

I need to register for something. Don't ask me what, but it was important at the time. I start to fill in the blanks on a company website. As I am entering the necessary info, my email pops into position in the box. Oh shit, it's spelled wrong. Now I have to figure out a way to delete it and start over. *Sigh.* O.K. Back on track. So far, so good.

I enter my secret code, and I am told in red print that something's wrong. I go back and try to correct whatever it is. Upon entering the magical code, a pop-up appears and states that all the printed info is not correct, or my secret code is wrong. *BTW, you shouldn't think this is going to go on for much longer, lady. Two more tries and you're history.* Oops. Sorry, try again later.

The *coup de gras* happens when you are finally on their website, push all the right buttons, and feel pretty smug and relieved about knowing all the answers. The end is in sight. Now, one of two things happens; either you get disconnected, or words pop up declaring, "You have been on too long," and it shuts off as the info on the screen goes to black with a pop-up message that says, "Good-bye." *Memo to self: hire an assistant.*

Persnickety people like kitchen counters that don't show the dirt. Fuhgeddaboudit! Show me the crumbs, and what's making my countertop sticky. Give me light tops; show me the dirt!

TEN

Just Say Yes

In the midst of an apocalyptic pandemic, radical racial issues, and an election year like no other, the year 2020 will forever burn up WikiLeaks. It will live in infamy in all historical venues as we in the United States, in my opinion, have become the Divided State of America.

Divisions run deep. Have we become incapable of meeting in the middle? Families, friends, split asunder, hopefully not forever, but only the passing of time will answer that.

Red States, Blue States, gray against the blue. Not since the Civil War of 1861-1865, the blood bath of brothers killing brothers, have we had such derision attempting to convince one side or the other, who is right, who is wrong, what is truth, what is an alternate fact? Alternate fact? History will record educated, and at times biased opinions for future generations to haggle over.

Voicing an opinion of one side or another will not move the needle of agreement, but one thing we all can be certain of; the level of stress will rise. Is having a stroke worth it? We need to address what works best for ourselves in order to stay sane…and healthy.

Just say yes. You meet someone, an old acquaintance, or new, and a discussion ensues. When having a dialogue with someone, let them talk, listen to their point of view. Control yourself. It's amazing how much more you both will get out of the dialogue if you don't break in, contradict, or interrupt. When they have finished with whatever was on their mind, stop, smile, count to five and then decide whether you want to give your counterpoint…or not.

If you do offer your opinion, hopefully, you will be respected and given the courtesy of being allowed to say what you want, without a challenge. Perhaps? Maybe? Probably not!

On the other hand, if you feel your stress level rising, fuck it. Speak your mind and/or opinion and walk away. Don't get into a rebuttal. Life is short; don't waste it on people who don't make you smile, and remember, most folks who wish to discuss or argue politics with you, will never make you smile.

ELEVEN

My Life is in Harmony

At this time will I pack in the suitcase of my life everything I want and desire in the indefinite time I have remaining? Does anyone? Our lives don't have an expiration date. At the age of eighty, I accept who I am, what I have, and am playing, '*Beat the clock*' for what I would like to accomplish. For one, I want to finish writing this book and see it in print, although I do not ever want to *finish* writing!

Everything is not for everyone. I recognize what works for me. My ABCs? Stay **A**lert, Stay **B**alanced, and be **C**omfortable.

I am thankful for knowing what makes and keeps me happy, content, and fulfilled. How satisfying it is to say it's more than I ever could have or would have expected!

I accept that what I have financially and for my future, is enough. I have prioritized my spending based on what is most important to me, (traveling). By passing up buying more clothes, how many tee shirts and sweaters do *you* have? (How many more do you need?), eating in fancy restaurants, or driving a newer car, I was able to build financial security. It's never too late to prioritize and start building your own nest of security.

I have a diversity of friends and relatives in my life; some in close proximity, while a host of others are out of state or out of the country. I stay connected with them virtually. Each one brings something special to my life, with their wit, sound advice, and love.

I am fulfilling my late-life with an unexpected enthusiasm for writing; fully aware that the end date is invisible as well as inevitable. Perhaps all things being equal, it's for the best. Although some stress and angst are unavoidable, mine mostly comes from the computer and inept techs from internet companies. Writing and seeing my feelings on paper helps balance what I consider my harmony.

The year following my divorce, lifting a line from Dickens, "Was the best of times and the worst of times." The best was discovering that I was somebody, that I count, that I can and do make a difference, and that people respect me. The worst was taking charge of my financial responsibilities.

In my divorce settlement, I settled. I should not have agreed to their offer. I didn't think it through. The entire experience was alien to me, fraught with a myriad of possible missteps.

I cannot emphasize enough that if you find yourself in a similar situation, take a step back and take a rest if you feel overwhelmed. Make it a point to fully understand everything presented to you before signing, and don't forget that fine print, and do not hesitate to ask questions. Be abundantly clear as to what you are agreeing to before everyone walks away from the table. Then move on, the best is yet to be!

TWELVE

I Traded my Husband in for a Gorilla

When I was in high school, in West Hartford, Ct., wearing long pants to school was verboten. The girls, wearing fashion dictated skirt-hems twelve inches from the floor kept their white bobby sox pulled up, although not quite reaching the hemline. This offered some protection from the frigid New England winters. We kept those sox from pooling at our ankles with rubber bands, which began to take their toll on the road to varicose veins.

We opted for the better choice of LePage mucilage and glue. This forerunner to good ol' Elmer's glue peeled off painlessly from our legs at the end of the day and had the added plus of impeding those aforementioned veins from looking like a road map on our legs.

Necessity being the mother of invention, keep your eyes peeled at Wal-Mart and Dollar Stores for new gimmicks. One glue especially became a game-changer for me. Throwing my weight against my bathroom towel bar and holding it firmly in place until it fused so securely to the tile wall, that I could swing from it, my thoughts swung back to all the time's something needed to be patched, replaced, or repainted.

"No, don't call anyone, I can do it." FLOML would mutter from his favorite position, stretched out on the couch like a weathering old caterpillar watching golf matches. *But when???*

You are now shit out of luck. You are stuck. Whatever needs his attention must wait until he wants to give it his attention. You are at the mercy of this other person that you are attached to, either by law, lust, or love. Who needs to continue sleeping with the handyman, a pseudo-contractor, at best, aka your husband?

Fast forward to the present and the new handyman on the block, Gorilla Glue. It will bond almost anything to anything; from bridges over troubled water to dental bridges and even your fingers if they should come in contact with it as you direct the ooze slithering out of its plastic container to your target. *Hmmm, if it supposedly sticks to "everything," how come it doesn't stick to the plastic bottle it is packaged in?*

Speaking of sticking around, and strictly as an aside, I don't know the statistics, but musing my own experience, I have a feeling that once a cheater always a cheater. *Once you know the thrill of the kill, it's hard not to kill again.* But you stick it out, haunted by those long-ago vows, for better or worse.

Another, *I can do it myself* invention is the over-the-door, thirty-six pair shoe racks that can hang on your closet door. It precludes being reliant on another to build more shelves or bending over for an interminable time searching the closet bottom for that one pair of shoes that goes perfectly with today's ensemble.

My latest Dollar Store find was removable hooks for hanging pictures. It's too high, too low, or not quite centered? With this handy gadget for the single lady, I no longer make a smorgasbord of nail holes behind my precious art.

When push comes to shove, hiring a handyman is more economical and stress-free when it comes to those tasks that require saws, hammers, and even screwing. It is definitely less frustrating than hearing your live-in promising, "I'll do it this weekend," always assuming his *quid pro quo* will be there as needed, i.e., prepared meals, clean laundry, and sex, whereas a good handy-man will hardly ever require prepared meals or clean laundry.

Adjustable wrench, a hammer (and sickle), a visit to Home Depot for your own personal pink tools, and, of course, don't leave there without a folding ladder. It should be no higher than you need to reach an eight-foot ceiling. Anything higher, you may want to have that handy go-to guy on your speed dial.

Today I went to my car dealer to have them look at my sun visor which drooped when I tilted it against the driver's side window. After a quick glance at the problem, my personal advisor had me sit in his mini-office while he clicked away on his computer for so long, I thought he was writing his own memoirs, seemingly forgetting I was sitting there. I couldn't help but wonder how many options could possibly be available for a drooping sun visor? Perhaps a well-placed paper clip or bobby pin could fix it?

Finally, he turned to me and gave me the news. It would be $215.00 plus tax for a replacement visor although there was absolutely nothing wrong with the visor; it was the doohickey that held it in place I explained that to him as though he was a first-grader.

"Nooo, the lining of the roof needs to come off," blah, blah, blah. My brain snapped shut during his elucidation of why this is how it's done, dumb lady.

Long story short, this dumb lady, through the internet found Robert, at Selective Auto, the first name to come up on Google for auto repairs. By the time I drove to his garage the temperature was a roasty-toasty ninety-five degrees on the blacktop driveway, so he invited me to drive ol' Lexy into his garage, where the shade helped to drop the temperature to a more reasonable and comfortable ninety-three degrees. It was almost as refreshing as jumping into a pool. He pried open the cover of the doohickey with a special tool, and looking at it with a flashlight said, "The screw fell out."

When the car was built, they obviously shorted the car one screw. After going back and forth multiple times looking for the screw in his screw drawers, he found one that came close to matching the original one, Voila! Robert hit pay dirt. After about one hour of me melting in place, he smiled, showing me the moving visor, no longer drooping when swung to the side.

"How much do I owe you?" I assumed they charged by the hour. 'Oh, nothing, I'm glad I found the right screw." I gave him a generous tip and promised any service that needs to be done to my car will be done by him. Then, in this time not of Cholera, but Covid-19, Robert proceeded to sterilize the inside of my car. He noticed my tires needed air, which he filled, after using Tuff Stuff to clean the narrow step inside the door. All this with a friendly attitude.

With good friends and family, the kindness of strangers, and no ties that bind with someone you don't want to be stuck with forever; you can relax and enjoy your ride on the tide.

THIRTEEN

Free-Dumb

Death, divorce, and moving are traumas that have proven to cause anxiety and stress. Stress can be a killer. You must learn to overcome it.

The physical separation of my divorce didn't cause me emotional stress. My meltdowns were brought about by having to learn to manage my personal financial responsibilities. The one upside of this is that I came to realize that "stressed" spelled backward is "desserts" so I knew I would eventually get through this.

What, me worry? I was in denial of financial awareness during more than half a century of married life. My standing joke to anyone who would endure my absurdity was that everything I bought was 'free.' This was essentially true, as I was never involved in the act of paying money for anything, as I was a profound expert in the use of credit cards.

All I had to do was hand over my silver-gray card and in return, I got whatever I wanted. It didn't cross my mind that the 'free stuff' was derived from my contribution to the family income via my seven-day workweek, selling real estate. The Amex card which, like the mechanical arm in a casino, dipped into our savings account every month and grabbed whatever dollars necessary to pay for what I got *for free* that month.

Thank you, autopay. It took some effort to learn how that procedure worked. I had too many meltdowns to count during the learning process. Here's how I thought autopay worked; I would put $2000.00 into an account for bills...I would have $2500.00 worth of bills. May the best bills win.

The system of autopay was in its infancy and wasn't as accessible nor as easy to set up as it eventually became in the perpetual evolving world of internet finances. After hours on the phone and struggles with the faceless accented voices of distant lands, I was finally able to consign my bank to pay my bills.

What worked for me was selling off and divesting my investments that needed daily attention. The less that things depended on "daily attention", the simpler one's life will be. Then I took this method a step further. I lessened those things that depended on "monthly attention" and then those that depended on "yearly attention."

After that, a whole new world opened up for me when I ended up putting the funds into lifetime annuities that get deposited into my checking account without any effort on my part, giving me peace of mind and allowing me to get *free* stuff again. I love free stuff.

Do what works for you. Don't take financial advice from me. I am mentally challenged in the world of finance. Once you figure it out, don't look over your shoulder to the world of should've, could've, and would've. Your investments may continue to grow after you cash out but think how smug you'd be if the markets went the other way. I'd rather make a little than take a chance to lose a lot.

What I did was right for me to eliminate stress and let me regain my sanity, even though there are still some folks who think I'm nuts!

All of my bills say "outstanding."

I guess I'm doing a great job with them.

FOURTEEN

Computer Chat

The electronic and computer age is constantly evolving. When prompted by a virtual voice asking the reason for the call and a highly impersonal instruction to "Press one" for a minimum of four choices that *he, she* or *it* seems unable to understand my Connecticut accent to direct the call to the proper department. That's when I start kicking and screaming, pleading to speak to a live; "Operator!", "Representative!!", "Associate!!!", and the latest one, "Counselor"!

Whew! Finally, I'm connected to a live person; "May I call you Brenda?" asks the voice, from a faraway country trying, oh, so hard, to sound midwestern, *I don't give a rat's ass what you call me*, "Yes." Their responses fluctuate from 'Awesome', to 'Very good,' to "Great' and now, (drum roll please), 'Perfect'. Yes, boys and girls, I, Brenda Frank have something I never achieved in school…perfection! Chantel won me over at *perfect*.

Our personal username and password criteria went from, *proof of identity* that needed to be at least six letters long, to at least eight letters, including a symbol and a capital letter. As of yesterday, though, I was told, symbols are OUT, but I can use up to twenty-five letters, making me ponder exactly which letter of the alphabet I would eliminate. Now there is something else I need to know, *internet identity*. Throw in a dose of pass-code and voila, you've got all the makings for a major migraine.

Hmmm, as I write this, shhh, don't tell anyone, but the next time I need to change ID codes; I've got it; *Majormigraine#1*. That should satisfy the password patrol.

Our passwords, for now, 'Can have no *cryptograms*'. I understand the first three letters of that funny word, cuz that's what I want to do, but I'm lost in space for the rest of it.

Even after Googling *Algorithm*, I am still wondering what the hell it means after being chastised that, "No, Al gore-isms are not quotable quotes from Al Gore." Light years ago, AKA three years in computer life, forces traveling faster than the speed of light had security questions that were relatively simple. The hardest part was remembering where they had been put for safekeeping, once I wrote them down; assuming I did write them down. I finally perfected my list and should have no problem getting into any site.

"What is your mother's maiden name?" In today's world, that question is no longer politically correct since we cannot assume we all have mothers, and if we do, they may not all be maidens. Today, the questions are as much a celebration of your recollection than of security. The last time I checked (yesterday), there is no longer one, but three questions to answer. My senior brain cannot assimilate and retain all this nonsensical info.

I needed to change my checking account and, *gasp*, and was required to set up new security codes at my bank. "What is your favorite song from your favorite Broadway musical and in what key was it performed? What day of the week did your longest living relative die? Who did you go to your first dance with?" The last one was easy. Joey Ferber.

Coincidently, I saw him at our sixtieth high school reunion. After he and I reminisced for a while, I told him he was part of my permanent security record. He was still smiling as he walked away scratching his head wondering who the hell I was.

Despite all these safeguards, why did I receive the phone call that my credit card had been compromised?

I suggested to the computer patrol that when they find the hackers, don't arrest them, hire them! These guys know better than anyone how best to safeguard our privacy if, in fact, we have any left.

FIFTEEN

All About Me

How did I earn the right to give advice.? G. Fox & Co., in Hartford, Ct., then one of the largest privately-owned department stores in the country is where I was well trained to be a salesgirl at the ripe old age of sixteen years.

Before being able to punch a time clock to start earning seventy-five cents an hour as a bona fide salesperson, all new employees had to attend a two-day training program. During one of those sessions, we learned how to give change. I realize that that particular talent is not so important today as long as the power stays on and the register spews out the change in the amount everyone happily assumes is correct.

How many cashiers know how to do that today, or need to, since most of us pay with a credit card? Don't count this skill out, one never knows when it may come in handy in the future. I'm sure you have gotten the look...you know when you are at a fast-food restaurant, your bill is $7.15 and you hand the cashier a ten, and fifteen cents. They proceed to tell you "That's too much," and wonder why you are shaking your head.

We were taught how to respectfully approach a customer, to assist them, and much more. To this day in my daily life, I still use what I learned then; simple manners, common courtesy, and the golden rule of doing unto others.

Five years later, as a wife and mother of two, I began selling original art. I peddled little handmade pewter figures and hand-made wooden toys at craft shows, made by others, and then fast forward to a stint as a medical assistant.

In Scarsdale, New York in the late 70's I was offered a job selling real estate. "Sure, I'll try it." *I'll stay until something better comes along.*

Twenty years into our marriage, FLOML became enamored with another. He told me about it after the bloom was off the rose. I was totally unaware of it since it's easy to lie to someone who trusts you. After telling me about his infidelity and swearing his devotion we moved on with our lives, somewhat the better now that he had lived out his fantasy.

While living in Manhattan from 1982-88, I was a manager for a rockabilly band, Ezze, *and the Manhattan Bay Trading Company* led by Sammy Fields, a well-known songwriter and musician par excellence. I secured a weekly gig for them at Dallas Bar-B-Que on W. 74 St. and had an open mic venue at O'Malley's on the east side of NY, which I dubbed, C.O.W.; an acronym for *Country on Wednesdays.* I engaged in all of this while maintaining top Realtor status, selling co-ops on Manhattan's Upper West Side.

FLOML got the itch to move every few years, and so we did.

Leaving show biz behind in New York City I continued selling real estate with every re-location; Yorktown Heights, and multiple moves from Miami Beach to Ft. Lauderdale.

And so, it went while I still waited for *something better to come along.*

At a Jewish wedding, the bride and groom sign a Ketubah, a contract that outlines the rights and responsibilities of the groom in relation to the bride. We promised to stick it out, for better or worse, in sickness and in health, as long as we both shall live. It appeared that he defined "stick it out" differently than I did. Signed, sealed, and delivered, even with witnesses. Quite a weighty commitment to make at the ages of eighteen and nineteen.

Well, after carefully reviewing it, although there didn't seem to be anything negotiable, he deemed it necessary, after fifty-six years to wiggle out of his obligations, and in 2014 he got the itch to ditch. *Adios Amigo.*

He scuttled out, leaving me on my own. In a very short time, lo and behold, *something better* came along. I attended a writers' group and became more motivated to write than to sell properties, sooo, I turned in my sellers' keys and locked the last door as a realtor.

Today I have never been happier as I sit at my computer letting my fingers catch my thoughts as they tumble out, advising my readers to let themselves go. You too may find, it's more fun to be a party of one than a gruesome twosome.

By dealing with people from every walk of life I saw how life was lived, from the lowest incomes to the highest strata. I witnessed people responding to life as newlyweds, coping with children, and of course, investing in real estate, which brings out the best and worst in people due to the strained emotions and financial burden of buying and selling. I heard their joys, sorrows, and fears.

Am I qualified to give advice? Yes, and even slightly encouraged, will do so. B.

SIXTEEN

A Letter to Myself

 Dear Brenda,

Life is like buying a coat. You try it on. It looks fantastic, and the color is perfect.

Except for one thing, it doesn't feel right. It's too snug when you move your arms. Take it off, try on another coat, or go to the next rack.

Life, like coats, has endless options. If one doesn't fit, move on and try another. Choose the one that's just right for you. Life is not about how something looks but how it feels.

You will begin selling real estate when you are thirty-five years old. It will be a stopgap until something better comes along. Never lose sight of that. It will take more than forty years, but something better will come along, and when it does, you will close your final sale.

You will find your passion. You love to write. You will discover, after being served divorce papers at a New Year's party at the age of seventy-five, that a bad memory makes for a good memoir.

My message to you, Brenda, it's NEVER too late. It's never too late to start over. Your opportunities are endless Most important is that you don't need anyone or anything to rely upon for your happiness.

If you don't think like that, you'll miss the boat, and you must admit, you'd rather be sailing on it.

Your older and happier self,

Brenda

SEVENTEEN

Friends

A running commentary I have through my stories is that I enjoy my own company. That does not preclude me from having friends and relationships. I love the men and women who are now in my life. I don't want them in my face, nor full time in my space, not at this time, anyway. I think that author Hans F. Hansen said it best regarding friends, when he said, *"People inspire you or they drain you...pick them wisely."*

It's liberating not having to answer to anyone. Married men are the men whose company I most enjoy. I keep it platonic. I am not seeking anyone's husband. I don't want anybody's boyfriend. I don't even want anybody's brother, although someone's uncle or cousin might meet my present needs. It works for me; no commitments, no responsibilities, no dinners, and best of all, no laundry.

EIGHTEEN

Being by Myself

As a young woman, I wanted someone to dance with. How much fun it would have been moving to the music in someone's arms.

For more than fifty-six years there was only one person that I loved. Is that normal? I propose the word *normal* be eliminated from the dictionary because what does it describe? It's a word that tells you nothing.

Ellen Goodman described "normal" as: "Getting dressed in clothes that you buy for work and driving through traffic in a car you are still paying for, to get to the job you need to pay for the clothes and car, and the house you leave vacant all day so that you can afford to live in it." I like my mother's definition better. When I asked her what was normal, she said, "It's just a setting on the dryer, honey."

Is it normal that I like being alone? I am not a hermit though. I interact with others enjoying interesting conversations with twists and turns, ups and downs, and diametric opinions. My mind is open to opportunities I didn't have for so many years and I am now taking roads I had not yet traveled.

The best part about being by myself is that I can release my thoughts organically. When I took my tentative first step into what I now call my Think Zone, I didn't find Waldo or Nemo, but I found me. I silently vocalize my thoughts, breathing life into the words I place prudently on the page, transforming them into thoughts, dreams, and fantasies that become my stories.

When I was working, my happiest moments, after endless hours of tedious daily responsibilities and commitments, was stepping into my apartment, turning the lock, and hearing that protective metallic click that separated me from the physicality of humanity. With a huge reduction now, in the number of daily obligations in my life, that separation has become my norm. I need that aloneness to be able to think within my quiet zone. I cannot connect with my thoughts if there is another in my space. I don't think this makes me anti-social, but rather pro-solitude.

Do I daydream or meditate? Is meditation a form of daydreaming? Does it permit your mind to float to a dimension of peacefulness, a way to rejuvenate, even if it's only short-lived due to the world that is always there… waiting with outstretched arms to embrace you on the other side of the door?

Today is the first day of another adventure in my life. I have turned my blinkers on, alerting those who are behind me that I am leaving the predictable highway, to travel roads into undiscovered territory. Most of all, I love the freedom which allows me to roam the world, whether in actuality or only in my mind, ferrying me to places not yet traveled.

NINETEEN

The Beginning of the End

B eing sued for divorce forced me out of my comfort zone and into one of utter mental chaos.

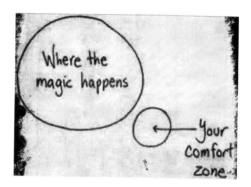

After paying him a substantial deposit, my attorney told me that I needed to list all my personal and household expenses and income. He did this while ushering me out of his office and simultaneously handing me a folder full of forms. The forms had to be completed by listing anything and everything coming in and going out. Huh? How and where was I going to get that info? Even years later, it's still painful to remember having to do it.

FLOML, since saying, "I do", did. He was responsible for paying the bills and taking charge of all financial matters for more than fifty years.

Assume nothing. I assumed whatever he was doing was okay. That's what a dutiful and trusting wife of that era did. When we didn't have money, what was there to think about? When we had money, well, what was there to think about? He made managing the household accounts seem complicated, but he was man enough for the responsibility.

I believe my lack of interest came from growing up with a very frugal mother. She ruled the roost. To get even a nickel, she was the 'go to' parent. If there was a theme song for mothers, hers would have been, *Pennies from Heaven.* I didn't want money to rule my life. As soon as I could, I joined the work force. "With money you get honey."

If I wanted something, I earned it, saved enough, and then bought it. I was a babysitter; not that I particularly liked babies, but there weren't too many options in the job market for an unskilled 12-year-old girl

When the *horse was out of the barn* and the legal un-entanglement began, I had no choice but to delve into the quagmire that is labeled "marital property." I live in Florida, where the law states, "The dissolution of a marriage creates equitable distribution." Don't believe it. Our distribution was anything but equitable.

In its simplest form, all money co-mingled between married couples is considered fifty-fifty, dividing all jointly owned property evenly. In my case, if the law was interpreted correctly, equitable distribution would have allowed me more than fifty-fifty, since I was the bread winner longer than he.

Our arrangement seemed to be, I made it, he spent it.

Everything I inherited from my parents, or money I earned, was split, fifty-fifty. I suggest you run, don't walk, and talk to your attorney and accountant, and make sure you protect your ass and assets. Speak to professionals you trust and know, and even then, get other opinions. Listen to those who have *been there, done that.*

In the long run not only are you protecting what is rightfully yours but having this legal information will move the separation process along quicker, saving you time and money. A lot of money!

Ed. Note: Things to watch out for: If things aboard the dissolution bus are rolling along smoothly and everything seems easy, please, "Watch your step getting off." Enjoy the trip; keeping in mind *trip* is the key word in this sentence. You may also trip and fall, trip and sprain your ankle, "trip the light fantastic," or take a trip to a place where 'No man's been before." Don't let your happiness be dictated by another. Make certain you stay in control of your life. And whatever you decide to do, don't get tripped up.

> **Happiness is an inside job. Don't assign anyone else that much power over your life.**

TWENTY

Sugar Babies

I don't deny myself whatever it may be that I crave, and throughout the years I seem to need less to satisfy these cravings. If I still want to eat a sleeve of Oreo's I will and wash them down with a glass of organic whole milk. The simple fact that I can eat whatever I want doesn't mean I will, but I don't punish myself when I want to satisfy my occasional longings.

My cravings have changed though the years, and desires to down boxes of cookies have been replaced. Today, knocking back one or two pieces of dark chocolate with almonds and coconut makes me happy. If I shake out all the food that has fallen into my keyboard, I could probably make a huge dent in the world hunger problem. Who knows what, or whom, will please me in the future?

Bet you can't eat just one…, anything loaded with crap. I don't want the food industry controlling my desire for food. Because of that I read labels, but if there is something that does reach out and beckon me, especially if I'm hungry, as I skip down the aisles of the markets avoiding bumping into people on scooters, I do stop and grab. Again, no deprivation.

The children of my generation were given food, usually sweets, as a reward for doing something that pleased another, or taken away as a punishment that bothered that same other. I read somewhere, the typical symptoms of stress are eating too much, impulse buying, and anything sweet. Are they kidding? That was my idea of a perfect day.

I turn on my TV upon awakening; any time from 5 to 7:00 a.m. After listening to the weather, I watch and wait to see if what I ate yesterday is still on the *good to eat* list. Caffeine, yes, today, no.

Eggs, butter, fat, no, yes, no, yes. It is a never-ending battle between food producers, scientists, and my cravings.

Lifesaving medications with a laundry list of side effects makes me dive deeper beneath the covers. I'd rather live with heartburn than get it from taking something that may relieve it but may also cause headaches, diarrhea, constipation, dizziness, thoughts of suicide and even the ultimate and often named side-effect, death.

It's not that I'm afraid of death, it's just that I don't want it to come as a side-effect from something that was supposed to help me. How would I explain that in the afterlife?

Try satisfying those cravings my way, a peppermint lifesaver.

What about the sugar? Oh, do you mean one of about fifty-six different varieties buried in the listed ingredients of all the food we eat? They are meant to do everything from extend shelf life to making food taste good. So, we'll eat more.

You get the appetite in the eating. How often do you eat when you're not hungry and then the taste of the food stimulates your taste buds? Before you know it, you have eaten past the point of being sated and half the bag of Oreo's has disappeared, while wisps of chocolate flakes float aimlessly in what's left of your glass of milk.

You are now uncomfortably bloated from over-eating. We know excessive eating leads to obesity and a myriad of conditions that come from that.

My heart aches when I see obsessively obese people. A losing battle for controlling their appetite is a winning one for the food and pharmaceutical industries.

Obesity starts in early childhood. Have you checked out the cereal aisle? I guess that the number of cold cereals that contains excess sugar is in at least the ninety-percentile range. Start kids on sugared cereal at an early age and you own them for life. Sugar is addictive. And a killer. When was the last time you swallowed Nyquil, with its thirteen grams of sugar in each serving…err I mean dose? Got some good sugar goin' in there!

A food ad caught my attention recently. The excited announcer exclaimed, no cornstarch, no additives, grain free, all-natural ingredients. I tripped over my slippers rushing towards the TV to hear better what he was hawking. Shit! It was Blue Buffalo Dog Food.

It's an uphill battle and the big guys are not our friends. For many of us, it's a lifesaving struggle. Make today the first day you use, as your daily mantra, the acronym *TACO;* TAke COntrol. *Hmmm, maybe I shouldn't use the word TACO as an acronym to control over-eating.*

After sitting in doctors' waiting rooms, waiting hours for a five-minute exam, if you receive that much attention, you then leave with the equivalent of a kid's lollipop. Your reward? You are given another appointment and a prescription, your prize for being…" Whooose a good patient!?"

I do not want to spend the last years of my life being one of big Pharma's chemistry experiments or attached to equipment to keep my ticker ticking if I may not be aware of where I am, who I am, or what I am.

TWENTY-ONE

Research Lab

How do you know you're ready to have sex, or want to have sex with somebody after a certain age? You are now a committee of one; therefore, you are also the chairperson and the only person you need to answer to.

When you meet someone, who knocks your socks off, don't miss the opportunity. A good icebreaker to acquaint this person with who you are, even if it's tongue in cheek, present yourself as a student of Masters and Johnson's; a person doing research, and let them know that the cheek is not the only home for a tongue. Or be a little more subtle and tell them, "Wow, nice pants…they would look great on my bedroom floor."

You could approach that special someone with, "Hi, there," I'm researching my book, *Sex after Sixty Sells*, would you like to buy in? Do you think people our age can have good sex?"

You might want to keep a journal describing the looks and responses you get after asking that question. You could also ask, "What do you think having sex is all about? Is it like two people enjoying themselves sitting side by side on a swing or the proverbial long walk on the beach?" If they answer that they think it is something like either of those, then they are not that "special person, and quickly move on to a new special person. On the other hand, if they happen to respond with something like, "What is a nice person like you doing in a dirty mind like mine?", they may be a keeper...for at least a few hours anyway.

That opening salvo beats other ways of self-introduction. In the beginning, getting to know each other and going through the courting or mating game can be time consuming and tedious. Why not *cut to the chase?* I ran into a gentleman at a friend's birthday party. He started the conversation with "Hi, I have a little blue pill and it has your name all over it." Intriguing and cute, but he didn't arouse any special feelings in me, so I moved on. I have my standards.

Is it imperative that you know all the intimate and historical stories at the beginning of what could become a lasting relationship? If you like what you see and you see what you like, go for it. Why not start a history of your own?

Today more than ever, opportunities are endless to meet prince or princess charming. Options abound through internet match sites, friends, social clubs, and where and when you least expect it.

Once you meet someone and you want to share an evening, wouldn't it be more fun to talk about music, current events, or sports; whatever is neutrally comfortable to you both? I suggest staying away from religion, politics, and personal history at the first meeting. Get together for the fun of it. Does it matter if the other person is divorced, single, or widowed? You are there to have a good time.

At the first meeting, must you interview to see how well you are suited for each other for a lifetime commitment? I will answer that for you with an emphatic NO. Wouldn't you rather have a fun time with each other and let destiny drive you to new destinations? Again, let me answer that...YES.

I would opt for instant gratification. Let the chips fall where they may, or, as Doris Day so prophetically put it, "*Que Sera, Sera,* whatever will be, will be."

If you enjoy your first meeting and a friendship develops, you'll have plenty of time to learn about each other; who they are, what they are, and where they came from. No personal information is necessary to simply have a drink or a dance or a stroll on the beach together for a pleasant, first time together date. Plus, it will give you something to talk about in those few awkward moments after a possible initial sexual encounter.

Everything is not for everyone. There is an art to a relationship. One thing you need to ask yourself is, *what am I getting out of it?* Never underestimate another person's entertainment value.

Not every relationship is as romantic as you may fantasize. No relationship is as idyllic as it appears to an outsider. Don't you find, with most of the couples you know, you would not want to change places with any of them? Would you really like to live with any of these men or women? Forever? If you answer, "Yes," then you have already crossed the line and shared some intimate moments or you would answer a resounding "No" when asked, "Would you want to be with one of them?"

Why Do I Write?

PART II

TWENTY-TWO

Why do I Write?

The metaphoric steam shovel scoops up piles of debris from my brain and dumps it. But, instead of dropping the heavy load into the back of a symbolic dump truck, it tumbles onto the computer in front of me.

Little did I know, when I started writing, not only would I enjoy the creative part, but the *re-moving* of my mental files and depositing them onto the written page would leave me feeling lighter and a bit exposed.

No longer am I carrying around the heavy weight of the past, especially any sad and cheerless stuff. When I read my memoirs it's as though that little girl I write about today is not me, but another little girl. The images of the path I traversed still resonate, but now my selective memory chooses to cast out the negativity. It vaporizes as it pours out of my fingers and transfers itself to the printing on the page and I create new memories.

When I was a wife and mother of two teenaged boys, in 1976 I was offered a job in the world of real estate. I accepted, with one proviso;

when something better came along, I would *jump ship*. Little did I know then that the cruise would be close to everlasting.

Lo and behold, after more than forty years as a realtor, newly divorced, my sons now married, I did just that. I discovered a love of writing, and my writing became a re-booting, and a re-grouping, as I re-invented myself as an author.

Is this a fantasy where one needs to be careful what one wishes for? So far, so good. I write what I see, do, touch, and feel. I hope to inspire and motivate others. Writing opens my eyes and my mind to seeing things in a philosophical, honest, and colorful manner. I write for the enjoyment and satisfaction of accomplishment. I hope to make an impact as I spell and spill my thoughts while breathing life onto blank pages.

Many people play golf, tennis, or bridge. How many of them presume they'll go on to the Masters or play competitively at Wimbledon? Or become professional bridge players? The satisfaction of accomplishing may be more gratifying than the accomplishment itself. Perhaps one day, I will write something worth plagiarizing.

When I started writing in earnest, my inspirations came in the middle of the night. I had to dictate them into 'notes' on my iPhone or they were lost by daybreak, or as quickly as I fell back asleep. By copying them to Word, my thoughts became the stories I wrote throughout the day.

I never imagined writing would be so titillating and stimulating. To give something of myself to others…whether to teach, enlighten, or even touch a nerve. To be able to make the reader laugh or cry; how good is that!

Who knew, when I started to write stories, they would turn into chapters which then become a primer; *Divorced After 56 years, Why Am I Sooo Happy?*

A bonus that came from my endeavor were the people I've met.

Men and women, on paths otherwise never to have crossed. Joining writers' groups in person and through the internet, meeting and sharing their same aspirations as my own, enriched my circle of acquaintances as well as facilitated my craft.

As crazy as it seems, I feel it's an out-of-body experience. My body sits at rest, while my fingers do the typing, creating something that didn't exist, as my mind dictates the story.

I eagerly await the next chapter.

TWENTY-THREE

Fried Head I Yam

My childhood friend Terry encouraged me to join a writing group. I was still selling real estate when my divorce, became final. My writing up 'til then consisted of tributes for deceased friends and family, and newsletters to homeowners. I never considered anything I ever wrote to be for the public. I was never inclined to write as an avocation.

On April 21, 2015, I went to a *Meetup* meeting where a group of hopeful writers in Hollywood, Fl.; six unpretentious men and women, were sitting around a large table in the teachers' lounge of a local school. Each one in turn read their original story. Listening to them, I was blown away by their talent. What creativity! How exciting was this? I wondered why I was even here, I wasn't good enough to carry one of their bags.

Nevertheless, with some prodding, I had the *chutzpah*, the nerve, to read something that I brought with me, *just in case*. It was a tribute I had written for my friend Bernice for her one hundredth birthday. They liked it!

On my ride home I thought, perhaps I should go to group therapy instead of a writer's group. If I go back next week, do I bring something I wrote previously? Would I even have time to think of and create something new and fresh in one week? One thing was certain, the thought of writing fiction was out of the question and how much personal stuff does anyone want to hear?

Although…the previous weekend, one of my girlfriend's had given me an electric hair ironer. I thought that was cool and was not at all bothered that it wasn't in a box and had no directions nor instructions included. I graciously accepted it for what it was, a re-gift.

Since I was a young girl, I had obsessed on having a certain style of wave on the right side of my head. I struggled with setting my hair the way it was shown in a ladies' magazine to achieve that sensual, Veronica Lake look. As an older teenager I was still hell bent to attain this look.

The results remained the same; abysmal and non-existent. Lo and behold, in the dimming twilight of my life my body got thicker, my hair got thinner and what was left of it became like the ocean, wavy. By now I was eons removed from craving the Lake look but, be careful what you wish for, regardless of my attempts to blowing it straight with a hair dryer, abetted by the Florida humidity, along with the waves, came curls. Think *Annie*, as in Lil' Orphan.

Hence the hair iron, aka straightener, was a great and welcome gift. I didn't give a thought to the missing directions. What could go wrong? How hard could it be to use something that millions use every day? How hard indeed. Only later would I learn that a warning label comes with all these devices alerting potential users: *Do not use this equipment on wet hair.*

On the morning of that first evening, I was going to the writing group, I decided to try out my new toy, excited with my new gadget. After plugging it in I set the heat on 'high'. Higher in my mind meant *the higher the better.* With elevating anticipation, I started to work on my hair, searing my scalp and my fingers in the process.

My freshly washed and damp hair connecting with the heat of the iron produced a, crackling sound and my tresses began taking on a limp look. Behold, the wave I struggled to have millenniums ago, but now unwelcomed, hung lifelessly straight...er. Regardless that it looked awful, I thought it would be 'fun' to see if I could, 'kill' all the curls. Using a spray bottle, I misted my fifty shades of gray and proceeded to iron the rest of my hair. *Snap. Crackle. Pop.* And that odd smell...what was that?

I dressed, did a head check; *pretty bad,* before locking my door, and proceeding to the elevator with its bright halogen lights that shine straight down. Yikes! Looking into the mirrors between the two opposing walls with my reflection repeated ad infimum put me into a slight shock of disbelief. I looked like a sheep that had run into an electric fence.

I had completely fried every hair on my head. Two lucky things were in my favor, #1 no one got on the elevator and #2 it was a very untypical Florida rainy day.

When I got to work, I headed straight for the, *when did this room get so bright* ladies' room? I patted the frizzes down with damp hands not realizing it was making matters worse. Throughout the day I kept peeking at my fried head wishing it to look better. That was the day that I confirmed that wishing only works in fairy tales. My fellow realtors, politely refrained from making any comments, assuming I was having a bad hair day, A REALLY, BAD HAIR DAY.

When I arrived at my first ever meeting of writers that evening, I took solace in the fact that no one knew me. Hopefully they would not think I just came from having shock treatment, although I suspected a few of them must have been thinking, 'Poor thing, better her than me.'

I arrived home after an exhilarating evening of being with authors, and before getting into bed I slathered my head with Argon Oil. I checked around 5 a.m., relieved my hair was still intact, but it was too oily to see if it still was fried.

Hoping it was not permanently damaged, I added conditioner to my lubricious hair, thinking, I couldn't do too much more destruction. If it looked as sizzley on Wednesday as it had on Tuesday, I would go to my favorite hairdresser Albert, throw myself at his mercy and let him do his magic: *off with her head, err I mean her hair,* and cut off the fried hair. If that failed, *Wig City* here I come.

With the oil and the added conditioner, I was a freakin' mess. I kept thinking of Nancy, from the old comic strips who had a round head of wiry hair. At least she had a full head of hair.

What to write? What to write? Don't overthink it, no pressure. As I was getting ready for bed peeking at my head one last time, I thought why not write my "gray head and fried" story? Even Dr. Seuss hadn't thought of that one. And this, my dear readers turned out to be the first chapter in my life as a writer.

TWENTY-FOUR

Everything is Not for Everybody

My stories are like a buffet in a restaurant. Read what you want and skip the rest. It's the reader's choice. Isn't that what life's all about, making choices?

One of my choices is to stretch. Whether it's to stretch my ability to write, stretch to reach out to someone for a new relationship, stretch my imagination, or stretch my goals, i.e. making changes so that I can grow.

What I have been doing for several years is stretching my spine, just a moderate stretch. I have a bar bolted in between the door jamb to my bedroom. I am not any kind of a therapist, but I do what works for me. You, dear reader, need to find what works for you. As I walk by, when I think about it, I reach up and hold onto the bar without pulling myself off the floor. I stretch until I feel my spine straightening. I do it for about ten seconds each time.

That makes me feel good. It seems to be keeping my sciatica in check, and so far, I haven't had much height shrinkage which I know will come a-knockin' regardless of my home remedy. This is not a major commitment for physical fitness but doing something is better than doing nothing. Each person needs to find what works best for them.

I turned my running shoes in for walking shoes. Walking while being ear-wired to my iPhone allows me to enjoy music of my choice or, if I want to learn something and get me thinking, I'll find a voice that teaches, "The difference between a cliché and a metaphor," or gets you thinking, while I click off the steps, which some of the voices in my ears are convincing me, are life extenders. I also 'do' yoga, which is good for my mental as well as physical well-being, so I've been told!

We spend half of our life collecting. The other half of our lives, getting rid of those *must-haves*, and that includes wives and husbands as well as the *tchotchkes*[1]. Like switching from Democrat to Republican, or gender change from a man to a woman or vice versa, my 'married' status flipped over to the divorced column. I became a new statistic. Now, when asked, "How many live in your household?" I answer, "One."

---

1. Knickknacks

TWENTY-FIVE

Don't Think It Doesn't Count

E arly one Monday morning, at the end of August, I went to the modest Sunny Isles Beach Synagogue a few blocks from where I lived, in South Florida. My mother had passed away in April and while going through some of her belongings I found a box containing my grandfather's tefillin, sometimes called phylacteries; a set of small black leather boxes, connected by leather straps. They contain scrolls of parchment inscribed with verses from the Torah, which are the first five books of the Hebrew bible. Orthodox Jewish men wear these on their arm and head during their morning prayers. I also found a small prayer book and a text written in Hebrew.

A kindly gentleman received me. I showed him what I had and asked if he, or someone, could translate what was written.

The paper was crumbly, fragile, and the writing had faded over time. He said it looked like it might have been written in Aramaic. He took time to attempt to translate the writing, but to no avail. I asked if I could pay him for his time, but he refused any payment.

"What can I do to repay you?" I asked.

Smiling he said, "Vote for me."

"Oh, what are you running for?"

"Commissioner of Sunny Isles Beach," He replied.

"You have my vote," I assured him. We shook hands and I left the synagogue with a light heart.

I never voted for him. Sept. 11, 2001, primary voting day. I woke up at my usual time, 7 a.m. and turned on the TV to *The Today Show* to watch the weather. I showered and got myself ready for the day, with voting being my number one priority. I didn't pay much mind to the TV. Matt Lauer and Katie Couric were bantering about nothing that attracted my attention, that is, until about 8:45.

Matt, looking very terse, and in a stunned voice reported that an airplane had just flown into the World Trade Center. By the time I wrapped my head around this, he announced another plane crashed into the second tower. Then came the news that two other planes crashed, one in rural Pennsylvania, the other into the Pentagon in Washington, D.C. My heart stopped; my stomach churned.

Stunned, I watched and listened to the news. In 2001 neither one of my sons had cell phones. I called Kevin at home in Brooklyn. He and my daughter-in-law had become parents of my beautiful granddaughter, Abbey, on June 22nd. No answer. I got their answering machine. I remember screaming into the phone, "Put the television on, do not go to New York!" Kevin worked for NBC and usually left home after rush hour.

I called my other son Jeffrey, who lived in Washington, D.C., leaving another frantic message hysterically on his answer machine.

I stayed glued to the TV. By this time, all three TV sets were on, on three different channels. I kept trying to reach my children. The phone lines were jammed. I was desperate.

I was in shock and numb from watching the horrendous events that were playing out, live, in real time, right in front of me. This had to be a nightmare.

Please, God, let me wake up. I know the Trade Center, I've been there, done business there, had dinners at Windows on the World.

WHERE ARE MY CHILDREN??? I silently shrieked. All the wishing in the world was not making them call me. My anguish was unbearable.

Barely breathing, I watched the horrific reports. The unknown news was just as sickening as what we were seeing. Finally, at about 2 p.m. I heard from Jeffrey; he had been riding his bike in the morning not far from the Pentagon, but far enough away to not be aware of the nearby tragedy unfolding in front of the rest of the world. He had tried calling me when he returned home and heard my frantic message, but all the circuits were busy.

As he left for work on the subway, Kevin heard the news while traveling under the Trade Center. Rather than returning home he stayed on the train, thinking that he might be needed at work at NBC.

Locked down and locked out he realized he needed to go home, but by now New York City had come to a standstill. The streets were crowded with stationary beings, looking like a tightly woven multi-hued carpet of people.

Kevin started walking downtown toward Brooklyn. Once over the Brooklyn Bridge, a policeman offered him a ride for, at least, part of the way home. My daughter-in-law, busy with her baby, hadn't turned on the TV and wasn't aware of any phone messages. The phone service was erratic, but I finally reached her. Kevin showed up soon after. My children were safe.

By this time, I was thoroughly spent. My thoughts were to go and vote, but in the afternoon, still bonded to the TV and usurped of all energy, I buried my palpable guilt and didn't go.

Early the next morning, after a sleepless night, I watched the crawl at the bottom of the TV showing the results of all the local elections. The results of the commissioners' race showed that the nice gentleman in Sunny Isles Beach who I had assured would receive my vote, lost the election…by one vote. One vote? You have got to be kidding me. I froze. No! Please tell me I read the crawl wrong. I waited for what seemed like an indefatigable time as the results from all the other cities crawled by. Here it comes. Shit! He DID lose; by one vote. My heart sank, I had an opportunity to make a difference and I did, but not the way I wanted to.

Besides watching and hearing the horrific stories from the day before, I was numb for not fulfilling my simple obligation and promise. There was absolutely nothing I could do about it. Along with all the other horrific news, I felt like someone close to me had died.

It was reported that afternoon that there was to be a recount in some of the districts, Sunny Isles Beach being one of them. I didn't want to hear any more. That evening I received a call from the vice mayor who was a friend of mine.

Before I could throw myself at his mercy and tell him my story and how awful I felt, he talked about the voting and why there was a need for a recount. He told me the recount was complete. My man, (he did not know that he was my man) lost…by two votes. My heart leaped.

Notwithstanding the tragedies of Tuesday's events, that news helped get me through one of the saddest days in U.S. history. The election news was the only news that propelled me through the long days and nights that will forever be emblazoned in my mind. The day our country came to a stop and the day I learned how important it is to count on yourself to do the right thing and, to be counted.

TWENTY-SIX

Highway One

Stashed away in my attic were stories lying dormant . . .

My secrets having been left in a locker decades ago that I didn't remember having been put aside as I traversed through life related and connected to others.

Released when I opened the door, and took a step out, closing it behind me.

What I left behind was the opposite of what I found ahead.

Upon opening the door, I took a deep breath of cool, fresh air.

My mind began to fill with self confidence and my sense of humor which makes me laugh out loud.

What more do I need for a bowl full of joy?

I am roaming on my metaphorical highway.

"Why?" I ask. "Why not", I answer.

Where am I going? I don't have a clue.

When will I get there? What does it matter?

What will I do when I get there? What difference does it make?

Life teaches us the journey can be more interesting, more fun, than the destination.

Well, here I am on Highway One or am I Highway One? Where is Highway One?

It's in my head ready to be released, no longer locked up, twenty-six characters in there, spilling, toppling over the matter that is my brain.

TWENTY-SEVEN

Mom

___

When I received the call April 8, 2001, I did not believe that my mother, this strong woman, at the age of eighty, was gone. ADams (23)2-5540 was my parents' BC, (before cells) home phone number for over fifty-years. That number, my lifeline to them for more than forty-three years after I left home to get married in 1958, will now pass on to another family.

I hope that whoever is lucky enough to be assigned that phone number will have a wonderful and full life. Newborn babies were announced from or to that number, the passing of grandparents and family members were sent and received from that number. Health updates were duly discussed ad nauseam. Close friends and family members constantly checking up on my mother the last six months of her life, reached her on her phone.

If we could capture all the conversations that were spoken over that phone, we would have the complete and unedited history of my family, the Ann and Buzz Simons dynasty. Despite some strained times, typical between generations at that time, my parents shaped my life. Mother loved to boast about her children to anyone who would listen, and even more about her grandchildren.

She was down to earth. I never saw or knew my parents to be jealous of anyone or anything others may have possessed. Materialism was not in her DNA. My mother was true unto herself. I took this with me when I left home.

My mother was strong. If anything would knock her down, she would get right back up, always regaining her center of gravity. The one thing that made her resilient, was the truth. She was a dedicated Democrat, and every election she volunteered at her polling place. She never forgot to tell me and anyone else within the sound of her voice, "You must vote. I don't care who you vote for, but you must vote!"

The last six months of her life, she suffered from an unidentified condition. As painful as it was for her to walk, she still managed to do so. She would uncomplainingly *schlep* to the markets and get her coupons tripled. She bought what was on sale and anyone visiting her never left without something she 'happened to pick up' at the store, usually toilet paper or paper towels. I think I also took this with me when I left home.

My parents left a living legacy. My older sister Lois and me, along with our husbands and our four children. I made my mother a grandmother when she was forty-four. I had some complications after giving birth and she came to my rescue, taking over the job of caring for my son Jeffrey. That was the beginning of a loving and caring relationship that develops between grandparents and their first grandchild. My mother and I agreed Jeffrey would call her "Nana." We were living in Elmwood, Ct. then, and Jeffrey was about fourteen-months old when we went to visit my in-laws in Ft. Lauderdale.

We arrived home a week later and were greeted by Grandpa and Nana. Mother, concerned that Jeffrey forgot who she was in the time we had been away, swooped him up and asked, "What's my name?" He looked into her face, gave her a big smile, and said, "Grammy", what my mother-in-law was called by her Florida grandchildren.

We moved to Florida shortly after that. When Mother would come visit us, she and Jeffrey loved going to the beach. He would say to her, "Let's go talk to people, Grammy", and off they would go, the sand kicking up at their heels. For almost forty-two years my mother was not only 'Grammy' to our sons but 'Grammy Ann' to all my kids' friends. They loved her for what she was, unpretentious and fun. With her sense of humor and sharp wit she could hold a conversation with anyone, and usually did.

One of the things she and my sons Jeffrey and Kevin had in common, the three of them left their marks indelibly etched in their respective high school yearbooks and somehow touched everyone they knew. They all were chosen class clowns in their graduating classes by their classmates.

Grammy Ann painted a paint-by-number clown picture for Jeffrey when he was born. From there she graduated to sketch books, oil paintings, and art classes. She never talked, (or bragged) about how her teachers encouraged her to enter competitions, but when she did, she won awards and began to have a following of collectors. That talent, I did not take away. My artwork is a bit more basic than mom's and seemed to be a precursor to my life in real estate.

Mom cared about people, and they cared for her. During her last days, as she was struggling to breathe, she still managed to ask and learn the histories of all her nursing aides. I hope I took that attribute away. As I am rounding the bend on my own life and reminiscing about her, Grammy Ann is still remembered today by my childhood friends who remind me of how she touched them and of course my children's friends who still laugh at some of her antics.

She worked in a children's furniture store and was respected as being hard working, sincere, and above all, honest. When expectant parents chose a certain crib mattress, she would talk them out of it if she didn't feel that it was strong enough, well-built enough, and even in those days without the safety measures in place today, would point out that they could be dangerous. She had an amazing following, and it is fair to say that most of the babies born in West Hartford during the time she worked at the Toy Chest in the "Little Folk's Furniture" department, slept soundly in their nurseries and baby carriages sold by her.

"Wanna try pot?" One of the young delivery men offered her one day, in the twilight of her life.

"What's pot?" After getting a tutorial about pot smoking, she, a Parliament two cigarettes a day smoker, was the first family member to smoke the then illegal substance.

"It was okay, yeah, it wasn't bad, but it's not for me." She preferred vodka.

My mother left the most valuable legacy anyone can leave; her good name and memories that others live to share, to pass on to their heirs, and those who never knew her personally, but will know she lived. She left a notable and heartfelt imprint.

AD2-5540 is a phone number that remains with me today; a lifeline to the world which I still remember almost sixty-three years later.

TWENTY-EIGHT

Funday in the Park with Josh

E veryone on earth shares the same fate. Ol' Father Time has no favorites. He's blind, deaf, and ignorant to who, what, and where you are. He can't be cajoled, bribed, or threatened. He doesn't play favorites. Like it or lump it, tick-tock, all living creatures have the same 1,440-minute 24-hour clock. One thing that never varies is the relentless passage of time. You can either sit idly by and watch it pass, or you can take time and run with it as you live out your dreams.

It's painful growing from a fertilized egg into something with a head the size of a cantaloupe and pushing yourself, as a camel passing through the eye of a needle, through the love canal.

Ouch. I'm leaving here, to go where? Through there??? Never gonna happen!

After living, do I have to go out the way I came in? Nope. That's a relief. Where do I sign up?

Enter with a cry, leave with a sigh. I've had many changes to adjust to now Since our *'til death do us part'* vow was nullified, and we will not be together for eternity where does the final piece of the puzzle go?

I've re-established and adjusted, happily, to my new station in life. Now, where will I settle down for the very last time? Regardless of where, I plan to be wearing my trusty denim burial skirt, the one that I have never left home without on all my earthly travels for more than forty years.

My dear Aunt Rose and Uncle Sam are resting in peace, or as they did in real life, still bickering, especially since Sam, who outlived Rose, remarried. Their final resting place, regardless, is the King David Cemetery in Lauderhill, FL.

My two cousins, Judy and Michael, Rose and Sam's children, as well as Cousin Laney came to visit me. Since neither offspring wanted them, this was an opportune time to check out the available burial plots the dearly departed had purchased before they departed. They chose to be interred, side by side in the middle leaving an empty plot on either side.

We four cousins and two spouses drove to the cemetery. After taking selfies at the site, we walked into the on-site funeral home and office. We were welcomed with the predictable Florida greeting by the predictable-looking sixty-something, plumpish receptionist.

"Good afternoon, how may I help you? Have a seat. Would you like some water?" She asked without taking a breath. Michael explained about the plot swap. Soon Josh, the funeral director, a serious-looking man in his forties, came out and escorted us into his office. He was wearing a lapel pin that simply stated: *My day begins when yours ends.*

When we cousins, our mothers were three of the four Weil sisters, get together we think we are *weilly* funny. No matter the situation, we find humor in it. Josh, bewilderingly befuddled by this senior band of vagabonds, didn't get our dry humor at first but soon caught on. This was not going to be the usual maudlin meeting for funeral arrangements. Firstly, we pointed out we were all here, at least physically, and not ready to be boxed up to go there, wherever "there" may be.

Michael started with an ice-breaker conversation, well suited for this occasion. He told the story of his petite deceased ex-mother-in-law sliding around in her oversized coffin as the pallbearers tried desperately to shove it into the fresh new concrete vault that had been made too small for the coffin. The mourners remained by the gravesite waiting for something to happen. The diggers left and returned fifteen minutes later with jackhammers, and hammered away at the vault, required by law that coffins need to be placed in. Grace was finally delivered and slid into her final resting place as the sun slid into the horizon on a chilly October day in Queens, New York. I reached over Josh's desk to close his mouth which had fallen open at this mortician's nightmare.

No tears, just facing the fact that dying and death are a part of life. By now, all of us cousins were trying to outdo each other in the wit department. Josh bragged his graves were forty-two inches wide, not the usual, run of the mill, thirty- six inches. We agreed that with this info, "We'll all sleep better tonight," knowing that an oversized casket would cause us no undue harm.

After signing the 'quit claim' deed over to me, and me paying him the closing cost of $50.00 Michael was corrected by Josh to the fact that extra lots were, in fact, salable to outsiders but the chances of getting someone, who was dying to want a single on the side of two family members, was slim to nil. Hmmm, I thought. Wait until Michael sees my marketing campaign. Perhaps I'll put a, for sale by owner tiny sign on my newly deeded tiny property, or list it on MLS, as I try to roll over my plot and buy one that allows you to have stand-up markers. Rose and Sam are in the section where all the markers lie flat for easy mowing.

Josh began asking me for vital information for my death certificate. "… And what level of education did you have?"

"Huh?" What does this have to do with settling an estate, I thought. None of us asked. I said we were funny, not smart.

We just stared at him until he inquired, "What is your title?"

I asked, "Whaddaya you got?"

"Ph.D.", he started.

I didn't hesitate, "PhD? I'll take it."

Heretofore, while my completed education, college courses here and there not considered, earned me a high school diploma you can address me as Dr. Frank (no en-stein after that please.) Waddah they gonna do after I'm gone; shoot me? Inaccuracies are made all the time. No one questions grave markers.

What did flash through my mind, but then I let it die, was being dressed and buried in my wedding dress, the symbolism being that I and my marriage were dead. Nah, that was going too far! He dutifully added to the form my instructions about my travelin' burial skirt. We left after asking Josh where to go for an early bird dinner. We all agreed to keep on laughing; it's good for the body and the soul, and besides, it stimulates your appetite. We toasted those loved ones over there to those who are still here: "Here's to everyone's long life."

TWENTY-NINE

Turkey Trot

Thanksgiving is the only holiday that doesn't offend anyone. That is, except for vegans, vegetarians, animal rights people, native Americans, and of course turkeys. But enough about them. Each one of us has something to be thankful for. One Thanksgiving, I gave thanks that I didn't get thrown out of the Publix supermarket.

B.O. (Before Organic), most of us ate an old-fashioned dinner with all the beloved foods and *trimmings*. The meal became traditional and one we have gobbled through for the last four centuries. Along with comfort food chock full of cholesterol, chemicals, and calories it is a day for, (or should be) a peaceful family gathering.

Gonna stick to the basics, which everyone, after complaining about how bad it is for your health, enjoys. Turkey, cooking and basted for hours in its own juices, after first being slathered with oil and sprinkled with salt, pepper, and garlic powder, begins to radiate an amazing bouquet that encompasses the entire house. When this happens on the third Thursday of each November, that is the proclamation that Thanksgiving has officially begun. Although, for most men, Thanksgiving begins when the Detroit Lions kick off, and the Dallas Cowboys end their game.

Real potatoes, mashed with copious amounts of butter and whole milk, are always a crowd pleaser. What would Turkey Day be without canned sweet potatoes covered with rings of canned pineapple? Each ring, topped off with a Campfire marshmallow, looking obscenely like breasts pushing up through the casserole dish.

Canned jellied cranberry sauce, even, after slicing, doesn't lose the imprint of the rings from the can in which they were once imprisoned. And the whole -berry one? That never misses to elicit the conversation starter, "Did you make this? Yourself?" Nope. Canned, again.

Aunt Gert always brings the sure-to-be show-stopping string bean casserole, canned green beans, stirred into Campbell's canned cream of mushroom soup, topped with greasy canned onion rings. String bean casserole became a traditional dish to be served on this holiday. This phenomenon came about in 1955 when the Associated Press included the recipe in its Thanksgiving edition. They implied that it was to be part of the annual holiday over-eating extravaganza and American's have bought into it ever since. Can you think of another time you even make it? I wonder if Native Americans, sitting at the groaning board with the Pilgrims, looked at their squaws, and asked the burning, probing ultimatum. "Why can't YOU make this?"

With all the guests seated, the *piece de resistance* is carried out, held high like a sacrificial lamb to *oooh's* and *ahh's* of the waiting gourmands as the browned, roasted bird is laid to rest in front of the host who is impatiently waiting his turn to be top dog. Pepperidge Farm stuffing piled high in a bowl sits next to the gravy boat.

Fingers crossed, I hope the gravy will stay warm enough to not congeal, since it's made from, mostly, fatty bird drippings.

Let the slicing begin! The host, confident, looking to impress the guests embellishes his carving with swashbuckling motions. During the slice and serve show, my mind drifted off to two days ago.

My foray into the Publix supermarket started on Tuesday, at 9 p.m. after a long and grueling day reassuring buyers to buy and convincing sellers to sell their real estate.

The store was almost empty of other shoppers. Great. I will get through my shopping quickly. I moved, effortlessly, through the aisles, checking off my listed items as I threw them into my grocery cart, finally reaching the refrigerated food section. There, in an upright, glass front freezer, filling the entire compartment, were big birds packed tighter than passengers on a Spirit Airline flight.

Upon opening the door, the warm moisture of the store hit the ice-cold carcasses which were encased in form fitting white plastic sheaths. Immediately, these casings began sweating. When I reached in to take a bird out, its skin-tight sleek, wet body bag I didn't have anything to grab onto. It slipped from my hands, onto the floor. I bent down to pick it up.

Oh shit! Nooooooo!! The freezer door pushed open wider, prodded on by the weight of the other turkeys that started tumbling out. I tried forcing the door closed. Being no match for the weight of the frozen birds, I watched, as if in slow motion as they all slid silently, one by one, to the floor.

"Hello, anybody home?" I called. Looking up and down the aisle. But alas, it was just me and eight headless turkeys. I stooped down to pick them up. Weighing in at about twenty pounds each, those wet, white shrink-wrapped corpses kept slipping out of my hands. The harder I tried, even squeezing them to get a grip, the quicker and further they slid away. It was like the English game of *Skittles*. They silently skidded down the aisle, bumping into one another pushing them further away. At this point, they had skedaddled halfway down the aisle. It was like I was Curling, or ice bowling with turkeys.

Finally, I landed one and, with difficulty, wrestled it into my cart. I was as sweaty as the turkeys which didn't help matters. What to do with the others? Show of hands. How many of you have ever tried to wrestle a slick dead animal in wet plastic shrink wrap, hold it over your head and stuff it into a front-loading freezer? On top of other animals? Finally! Success! I got one back in. As I struggled to get another one on top of that one, the bottom one slid down and out. Fuck!

I was tired, hungry, and sweaty. When I get tired, hungry, and sweaty, I get a runny nose. Rummaging in my handbag I was able to find a used Kleenex. My wet hand shredded the tissue as I tried removing it from my bag. Think! *What aisle is the Kleenex on?*

I started to take my leave of the birds, that were now able to be legitimately labeled as *free range*, to look for the paper aisle. I left my cart in place as a collateral offering, validating, with its unspoken message that I was not leaving the scene of the crime; I had every intention of returning.

At that moment, a store employee appeared. The young man looked, with wide eyed disbelief, at the bird covered aisle, and then turned and stared at me; disheveled, wet, and wild eyed with a runny nose. Giving himself few seconds to assess the mess, and compose himself, he asked sympathetically, "May I help you?"

After my debacle, turkeys are no longer held captive in upright freezers. They are in open, cold floor bins where one can lift their bird of choice out without having to chase them down an aisle. It is possible that my experience with those frozen turkeys supplied the impetus for the turkey packagers to add the ever-popular mesh and carrying-handle on all frozen turkeys.

You're welcome.

THIRTY

Elsie

M y friend Elsie confided in me something I had thought about but would never ask her. What DO they do all day? Every week for more than five years, Elsie welcomes a gentleman caller. Hal makes house calls to her home every Sunday.

After a visit, the two of them drive off together to have lunch, usually at a local diner. They then return to Elsie's home to "rest", for the remainder of the afternoon.

When I suggest going to a movie or a visit to a museum on a Sunday, she always has a ready excuse. Then she confided in me that Sundays were, in fact, "Hal days."

Recently, she and I spent the day together. She asked how my writing was coming. Little did I know at that moment, her story would become a story worthy of retelling. I told her, "I am letting the journey of writing take me to my destination. Some of what I write may be helpful, some are stand-alone stories, deemed to be entertainment for their own purposes, but perhaps my readers may find relevance in them."

After having lunch together in a local bistro, Elsie invited me to her home, eager to fill me in on Hal days. "You know, most of my friends are gone," Elsie began, as we sat on the flowery chintz sofa in her comfortable family room, overlooking a shimmering lake, "and at times I get lonely."

"Why not move into an adult community?" I asked.

"I've been alone for the last fifteen years since Bernie died. I've lived in this home for almost fifty years. If the walls could talk, what stories they would tell. Uprooting a half-century of life and memories would be daunting; physically and emotionally. Besides, I cherish my privacy. I don't want strangers watching me. You know, Bernie and I had a unique relationship. Oh, yes, we had our arguments that led to slammed doors and walk-outs but when all was said and done, we had more to give each other by staying than by leaving. Bernie and I shared something very special. We both loved sex. Why do you think, when we traveled, we never went with other couples?" I shrugged my shoulders, not knowing where she was going with her story.

"We went to sex clubs and erotic events around the world. Over the years we discreetly asked our close friends if they would be interested in traveling for fun and gratification. We received embarrassed and awkward sideward glances as they looked at us as if seeing us for the first time when we asked if they wanted to participate and share the experiences we did, to please our overripe libidos. Although nowadays people Google their innermost fantasies and can find countless online sites, from displaying an array of sex toys, to hooking up with other like-minded folks on media meeting sites. Computers are not my thing," Elsie continued. "I'm too old to learn new tricks if you catch my pun!" she said with a snicker. I listened to her story intently, taking mental notes as she continued.

"I still love and need to have sex. It doesn't take much for me to have an orgasm. No matter how, ahem, (clearing her throat), mature we women get, our fountains of youth continue to flow. A man, not so much, but there are ways to skin the ol' cat."

I sat there, riveted, trying not to squirm or look uncomfortable. I was fascinated, in a vicarious way, and wanted to hear more, but at the same time wanted her to stop. Sort of like heavy petting, I sheepishly, but salaciously, thought to myself.

Elsie is a poster girl for having sex as a healthy alternative to the *Stairmaster*, or any workout machinery for that matter, as well as partaking in the latest fad diets. She wears her age well and other than some creaking of the joints, she is in excellent shape, has a healthy glow, and always sports a smile on her face.

Perhaps, I thought, with the advent of robots, she can treat herself to a *Sex-Master-1*, delivered in an unmarked carton; no longer a futuristic fantasy, but available today online so she may no longer have to wait for Sundays to roll around; in order to roll around.

She continued to describe her Sunday with Hal escapades. *This lady IS hot*, I thought. Her boyfriend just needs to show up and lie down. She takes charge and achieves multiple orgasms for herself, while pleasuring Hal, and making him a happy camper as well.

Her story reminded me of an old advertising slogan; *Go Greyhound and leave the driving to us.* Elsie, detailing their visits, is happy to do her own driving, bringing herself and Hal to a climax, assuring her that Hal does not need to try other bus lines to reach his destination. Her passenger, younger than she, by sixteen years, has been loyal to this company for more than six years.

As she continued with intimate details about her Sunday *tete a tete*, a song popped into my head. Sally Bowles, warbling near the end of the Broadway show and movie, *Cabaret*. The name, Elsie in the song is purely coincidental. (I paraphrase)

> *The neighbors came to snicker,*
> *…that's what comes from too much…liquor.*
> *…When I saw her laid out like a Queen*

She was the happiest corpse, I'd ever seen.
I think of Elsie to this very day
I remember how she'd turn to me and say,
What good is sitting alone in your room
Come to the cabaret, old chum
And as for me,
And as for me,
I made my mind up back in Chelsea,
when I go, I'm going like Elsie.
Start by admitting from cradle to tomb
Isn't that long a stay
Life is a cabaret my friend
…and I love a cabaret.

My visit with Elsie inspired me. It will still be a memoir about the trials and tribulations of living on my own, and, by the way, I wouldn't want it any other way, but now it will also include personal stories about seniors that are sure to make their great-grandchildren blush.

Elsie celebrated her 96th birthday and I, along with a few friends were there to watch her blow out her candles while Hal waited his turn.

THIRTY-ONE

Dating is Not for Quitters

Not having had a date for more than fifty-six years, I was unaware of the social changes that have been imposed upon us in reference to senior dating. Contrary to the common belief that dating is like riding a bike; don't believe it. Neither endeavor comes naturally after a long absence.

A friend of mine asked me to go bike riding and I sure in hell was not hopping on a two-wheel bike after not riding for about forty years and saying, "Wow, that's true, you never forget." Even if you don't forget, would you actually try it? Without training wheels? Caution: at an advanced age bones no longer mend without the help of metal pins so, FYI, now you will be slowed down getting through TSA.

Age be damned. I have more energy and *joie de vivre* than when I was thirty and hankering for a nap every afternoon. Do you know what ages you? Boredom, stress, and illness. I'm not bored, and anything that's even close to stressful, instructs my brain to operate as a flood gate; allowing the stress to flow out and then slam shut like a bear trap. Just remember, sometimes we allow ourselves to focus so much on what amounts to "nothing", that we end up making the "nothing" into a very big some-thing. I will myself not to get sick. Try it, it works- most of the time. I want to check out, although not any time soon, while I'm healthy. I'm here for a fun time, and I'm determined to not spend my remaining time sitting in doctors' offices.

So far, I'm like one of those steel balls in a pinball machine. I stay in motion. As soon as I start losing steam and aim for the final hole, life flips those little flippers on the sides of the machine, sending the steel ball to the top of the game and into motion again. As long as life keeps prolonging the game and continues flipping, I'll keep rolling.

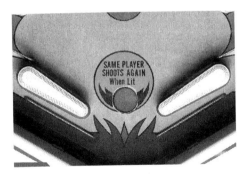

Most men beyond a certain age have difficulty in keeping up with me, even doing something as simple as walking. What does this have to do with the fact that I hadn't had a date, in like... forever? Nothing...really.

Regarding my own limited experience, I learned the number one rule for successful and stressless senior dating is for both parties to carry credit cards. That simple rule eliminates any chance of one or the other feeling that they owe or are owed anything by the other. It's a great rule at this stage of life. What I'm saying is to pay your own way, or give the impression that you are willing to, and capable of, paying your own way.

I've written profiles for my friends to post on dating sites. Although one should only write about what one knows, with my limited and very out-of-date knowledge I took the plunge and wrote about it, regardless. Hey, don't priests give marriage advice?

After listening to my neighbors' stories, the next story I wrote turned out to be as much fact as fiction.

Turn the page and meet Mary and Barry.

THIRTY-TWO

When Mary met Barry

A woman was sitting alone on a bench in the park when a very disheveled man sat down next to her. She started up a conversation. "So, how are you doing?
He replied, " I'm just out of prison"
"Oh."
"Yeah, I was in for twenty-five years. "
"What for?
He answered, "I murdered my wife."
"Oh, so you're single," she replied without missing a beat.

Unattached men are referred to as eligible. Women on the other hand, when they are single, are...well... single. It's a man's world...it's the boys club and there are a multitude of advantages to being a member.

Statistically, men are in the driver's seat. Too few of them to go around. It is believed that women outlive men due to a combination of biological and social differences. It seems that male testosterone is directly linked to a decrease in their immune system, which raises the risk of cardiovascular disease as they age. I believe it also has to do with the fact that men have historically been involved in basically doing stupid things. Because of the high demand, men set the rules for the women who outlive them.

Gloria Steinem and Betty Friedan, two leaders of the modern Women's Lib Movement, broke through the ceiling of hard knocks in the 1960s. Women born before the early '60s relied on the opposite sex for their financial security and most of the decision-making within most relationships.

It was a man's world, while a woman's place was in the home. In public, people would look askance at a woman without a gentleman escort. A lousy dinner partner was better than sitting home alone.

Society tends to overlook even the biggest negatives men may have, especially being boorish, which covers rude, loud, and obnoxious. Looks?

Well, after a certain age, men and women start morphing together. It's not so easy to find a man that's not portly after the age of seventy. So, let's not even go there with that. Eyesight? You may have to pass on that evening drive. Hearing? Eh? Maybe he can hide it by reading lips. Ego? Well, let's just put it this way, *if men's penises were as big as their egos, there would be countless more happy females.*

Younger women, brought up in the already established women's lib era are no longer insecure about being seen alone in public, even, *gasp!* on a Saturday night. They replaced their tolerance for churlish men with a furry animal, either an aloof independent cat or a puppy that women feel compelled to put in a doggie carriage, rather than allowing them to walk and sniff as nature intended since the dawn of civilization. The following story depicts courtships that began fading away, thankfully, by the mid-2000s.

When Mary met Barry - First Date

Mary, a seventy-two-year-old widow, originally from Baltimore, was excited. Maureen, her hairdresser at *Supercuts* had arranged a date with Maureen's neighbor, Barry, a transplant from Queens, New York, and that rarest of breeds, a recent widower.

It was May 2015, when Mary confided to Maureen that she missed having a man in her life. She longed for male companionship. She desired someone to go to dinner with, take long walks, split a bag of popcorn at the movies, and of course the ultimate senior delight, a stateroom for two on the newest cruise ship. She loved cooking, but not for one, and had a fondness for buffet dinners out at sea.

Three days later, Maureen called Mary to say Barry would take her out. Mary had a week to prepare. She immediately sprang into action. *Hmmm, New hairdo, maybe a different color. Perhaps a shot of Botox or shots of the latest face craze quicker-picker-uppers. Of course, a trip to the mall to see the latest fashions was a must. A new frock or slack-set may be just the thing to turn back the clock.* We all know though, that clocks do not have a reverse gear.

Barry pulled up to Mary's condo and told the valet, "Don't park it! I'm just picking someone up and will be right back." Barry, alone now for seven months, was tired of eating take-out in front of the TV, where he has seen every episode of *Law and Order*, and boy, did he dread laundry day at the condo. It was always a *crapshoot* to find an empty washer and, a clean one, at that.

Barry was not quite as tall, nor Mary as short, as was expected, and neither was as young-looking as Maureen had described them. Barry was unaware that the unspoken dress code did not allow for short sleeves with a pocket. He could've at least lost the pen, secured to the pocket saver that left one black dot on the front of his light blue polyester shirt. *Where are the fashionistas when you need them?*

Pants, where should they be belted? Below or above a portly belly? The floodwater length pants are most unflattering. Oh well, nothing Mary couldn't fix, and evidently, there is a right and wrong way for portly men to don pants.

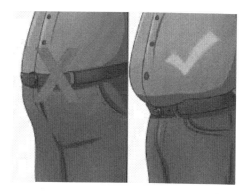

Upon arriving at the Sole Gourmet Café in Dania Beach, the walk to the restaurant wasn't any farther than a half-marathon. You could hardly expect Barry to pay five dollars for valet parking when there was a perfectly fine, almost empty parking lot directly across the street. And best of all, it was free.

Seeing that it was a hot, sunny day, the walk made Mary's feet swell up in her new, two-inch-high, open-toed, beige pumps. By the time they got to the restaurant her big toe, after being crammed into the shoe like Vienna sausages in a can, polished a shiny teal, had poked through the peek-a-boo opening, begging to be freed from the tight little hole. She tried not giving in to the pain from the non-stretchable *pleather* shoes and hoped she wasn't limping.

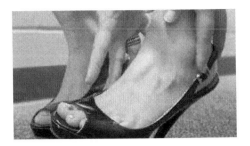

They were greeted and seated by the attractive hostess. Sashaying, she led them to their table. This did not go unnoticed by Barry, who was watching her derriere, rather than where he was walking. He bumped into a diner who was sipping her too-hot coffee. He hesitated, *don't cry over spilled milk,* or in this is case, spilled coffee, *in the middle of your lap on your white linen dress. It should wash right out.* and then apologized "Oops, sorry, Madam"

With a big smile, the hostess placed the oversized, not too clean menus on the plates already on the table and pulled out a chair for Mary. Sitting down, her neatly coiffed, blonde, more air than hair, teased and sprayed in place, felt as though it was being lifted by the breeze of the fan directly above them.

Grin and bear it, or change tables? Barry's hair that took him a half-hour to plaster across his shiny pate was beginning to come unglued from the sweat of the walk and now with the fan blowing he thought, *no, don't tell me, those strands are going to lift off.*

Mary, looking sweetly at him, asked, "Is this table okay?

He answered, "Are you okay with it? Their internal grimaces went unnoticed by each other, neither wanting to make the decision to change tables, so there they sat. Her hair continued shifting *en masse* with the motion of the fan and his plastered strands, now unglued, began waving like those oversized Gumby balloons at a used car lot.

Barry ordered first. "I'll have (tap) water and the afternoons' special. Chopped sirloin, well done, mashed potatoes, and cooked mixed veggies." Mary ordered a fresh, crispy veggie salad.

Although she preferred to order something more filling, she did not want to seem, not only too anxious but also not too hungry.

The water came and a short time later, their main dishes arrived, but not before the bread and butter. "We need more bread" barked Barry to Steve, their server. "Just bring a basket of loaves, and a sharp knife," he yelled as the waiter was leaving.

"Right away, sir."

Slathering butter on his second baguette, waving his knife, as though conducting an overture at Carnegie Hall, helped accentuate the opinions he readily proffered...unasked. This is all about him. Who he is, and most importantly, what he was.

Regaling Mary with stories from his past, she wondered, *is there a man out there, over the age of seventy, who was not the CEO of a no longer existent company? Is it possible they put that business out of business?* His eyes filled with tears as he told her about Joan, the love of his life for forty-six years. Did he forget or deliberately omit the time that he had an affair for three years with his dry cleaner's wife?

Their food was served. His is too cold and not well-done enough. Her salad is warm and wilted. Barry tried to catch Steve's attention. Steve has *waiter's eyes*. We have all experienced this. Try as you might to get their attention, without having to scream out an aria, or trip them, diners become as invisible as the wind once they've been served. Your waitperson shows up when you are halfway through eating, solemnly asking, "Is everything ok?" While they're really thinking is, *Is anything ok?*

Barry demands his plate be sent back to replace the cold one, disregarding that he has eaten almost half of his meal. Mary decides her salad isn't as warm and soggy as she thought and murmurs, "This is fine." Barry continues his diatribe as he waits for his meal to be returned, speaking louder than necessary, aware he has the attention of others.

With his meal replaced, he continues to brag, oblivious that he's spitting out chewed chopped meat, talking as he does, with mouthfuls of food. He displays the manners of a Viking at a pillaging party.

They decline to have coffee, being that "It's too warm" and pass on the tempting desserts as being, "too fattening."

Mary listens intently as his lifetime success stories wind down and the check is placed in the middle of the table. It's obvious Steve has been down this path before. Assume nothing when it comes to who is paying. Barry hesitates for an uncomfortable few seconds and then picks up the check ... $23.83. He plunks down $25.00, and loudly announces to Steve, "Keep the change", as obvious embarrassment covered Mary like a blanket of steam.

The best part of dating is the grand entrance and leaving from dining establishments. As Barry escorts Mary, weaving between other diners, Mary is pleased to impress all lookers that she is attractive and desirable enough to be with a man.

She cooled down enough to have her feet go back to their original size, other than the blister that formed on the toe that wanted so desperately to escape its petite confines. Walking thru the restaurant was not as painful as the walk in. Hmmm, this could be the start of something good.

When they reached the door, Mary told Barry that she had left her phone at the table and ran back to leave a five-dollar bill on the table. She felt much better for it.

Mary and Barry walked out into the mid-day sun. Not wanting to appear weak or needy and having to ask Barry to pick her up, she decided she could survive the walk to the car. She really couldn't. Her feet started to swell up right away and oh, that toe, trying so desperately to get through the hole. It was now twice the size as the shoe. After securing her seatbelt, Mary began to wiggle out of her shoes. The left one came off easily, but oh, the right one begged for some type of extracting tool.

Barry pulled out of the parking lot as Mary leaned down to take her shoes off. He did not see the car coming towards him on his left side. As the car skidded around them, Barry slammed his foot on the brake and came to a screeching halt. Seat belts be damned, Mary's head hit the dashboard with a thud. Barry looked over and said to her, not, "Are you okay?" but, " What are you doing?" *Holding my head, you stupid ass. Can't you see that?* She impulsively thought.

A huge blister had formed where her big toe was. It looked almost like another toe growing out of her existing toe. She began to feel her fore-head tighten. When she pulled down the sun visor to look in the mirror, she wasn't surprised to see a walnut-size knot.

Barry was sorry she had hit her head and woefully admitted he had not looked to his left when he drove out of the parking lot. For a second, he thought, *oh shit, why am I saying this? She may wind up suing me.* Nahhh. Glancing over, he saw she was preoccupied with her feet and not mentioning her head. *Hey, does she have six toes on her right foot? I should have checked for that earlier.*

The rest of the ride back to Mary's condo was uneventful. They made small chitchat about the restaurant, the food, and the service. As he was pulling up to the front of her condo, he couldn't help but notice that she wasn't wearing shoes. He was relieved that she was more concerned with her feet than the bump on her head. She smiled at him as she got out of the car and told him what a good time she had had and hoped that they would see one another again.

Barry didn't say much. Walking around the front of the car to his open window, she leaned over and gave him the ultimate invitation. She invited him to come for dinner one evening, or because of the night vision issue, one afternoon.

Well! Nothing like a home-cooked meal after not having one for seven months. This could be the start of a beautiful romance.

When Mary met Barry - Second Date

The Saturday after their lunch date, Barry was on his way to Mary's condo for dinner. He looked forward to seeing her again and anticipated a pleasant evening and more importantly, a home-cooked meal. Since his wife Joan died suddenly of a massive heart attack, his eating habits were quite grim. He had learned the intricacies of making his own Kraft Macaroni and Cheese dinner and had one Chinese and one Italian restaurant on speed dial.

He was feeling good about himself. On the way, he had stopped at Walgreen's to buy ear wax remover, and lo and behold there, at the end of the aisle, was a bin filled with Easter candy, 75% off.

At the agreed-upon time of 6 p.m., Barry arrived at Mary's condo. Mary's limp was almost indiscernible as she went to answer the knock on the door. Barry came in, giving her a kiss on the cheek. As he handed her the post-holiday candy, he scanned her condo.

Not bad. The living room was decorated early 1980's. Mary had bought the condo ten years previous, completely furnished. The floor was fully tiled with twelve-inch beige tiles. Over this, in the middle of the living room was a faux oriental rug. Her Natuzzi, beige leather sectional sleeper couch had scarves thrown over the areas that had worn out or split open. A brown Barcalounger sat in the middle of the room facing the fifty-six-inch flat-screen TV. The sight of the TV visually aroused Barry. The glass end table, with the gold metal frame, discolored from oxidation from the salty tropical air, matched the cocktail table in front of the couch.

On the tables and on most surfaces, were artificial flower arrangements and some Lladro knock-off figurines.

Mary showed off her kitchen. Her fridge was covered with pictures secured under magnets bought in cities and countries worldwide. A great place to show off your family while covering the rust stains.

"Can you believe it's not granite?" Mary exclaimed, of her granite wannabe Formica countertop, as she gave Barry a *Cook's Tour* of her home. She showed him the half-bath, all decorated with frilly towels. "This is the powder room." In the full bathroom, being pleased with herself, she boasted "Look at the bathtub, it's like new!" It was. Mary took showers, downstairs in the ladies' gym. Barry noted that Mary's toilet looked like it had just gotten married.

Her bedroom held a king-sized bed which filled one wall. The Formica furniture was a pale beige, having oxidized from its original bright white, some thirty years ago. Sitting on her dresser was a forty-five-inch flat-screen TV. Barry's state of arousal visibly increased.

Beige vertical blinds covered the windows and the sliding glass door, which led to a balcony on which sat a wrought iron café table, two chairs, and an aluminum lounge. On the far wall, in a recessed alcove, was a stacked washer and dryer, something not allowed in his condo that he really missed. All in all, homey and best of all, clean.

"Hmmm, something smells good", said Barry, salaciously.

Having discussed their eating habits at lunch, Barry told Mary, "I eat and like just about everything" when she asked what he liked to eat. Through the course of their conversation, he proceeded to tell her he was lactose intolerant, border-lined diabetic, (along with being overweight), suffered from heartburn, wasn't crazy about fresh veggies, and hated fish. Oh, yes, he also had acid reflux, high blood pressure, and high cholesterol. Aside from those annoyances, though, he was healthy as a horse and "can eat and like just about everything."

Considering what he had eaten on their first date, Mary decided not to go too far afield from that. She invited Barry to sit at the dining room table which was covered with a pale green plastic tablecloth. The table was uncovered once, and that was when the Realtor, who showed and ulti-mately sold Mary the condo, peeled back the protector. Being that it never was exposed to the light of day, the walnut veneer was as good as new and shined like a brand-new quarter. The four dining chairs have seen better days. The stains and fraying were covered with small fingertip towels, albeit they got bunched up when sat upon.

She made meatballs, creating her own version of *boeuf bourguignon* using ground chuck, "It's tastier than sirloin,'" instead of cubed steak. "White or red?' Mary asked.

"White...red gives me a headache." Trader Joe's Pinot Grigio was chilling in the fridge. Its plastic screw-on cap made the necessity of a corkscrew redundant. It would make for a pleasant complement to the stew, with its fancy foreign-sounding name. At 6:30, dinner was over, even with them both having seconds.

"It's decaf?" Barry asked when offered coffee or tea.

"Yes."" How about having the *post-Easter* candy with it and we can watch the evening news?" Mary queried. Barry settled into the Barcalounger as Mary opened the box of chocolates.

"Oh dear." The chocolates had a greyish hue-aged tinge to them. They looked much like semi-smooth river rocks or a piece of flint.

No comment from Barry as he fussed with the TV remote. Having made himself at home, he clicked on the channel of his choice, FOX.

Mary, set the candy on the end table, putting the lid on the box of grey sweets in order not to embarrass him. FOX was not her news source of choice, *but what the heck, I can catch the local NBC news at 11.* Mary excused herself, but Barry appeared not to have heard her, engrossed as he was in listening to the latest 'fair and balanced news.

Putting the hot cups of decaf on a tray along with some Lorna Doone cookies, Mary started out, only to stub her sore toe on the threshold between the kitchen and the living room. She was able to catch herself and keep from falling, but in doing so, she dropped the tray, splattering coffee and cookies as the cups crashed to the tile floor.

Barry looked up. "You okay?" he asked. Not waiting for an answer, his head swiveled back to the TV, as Tucker Carlson held him in rapt attention.

"Yes," Mary answered, somewhat disappointed he did not make any effort to get up and help her. Barry was absorbed in the news as Mary cleaned up the broken cups and mopped the spilled coffee and crumbs. Her toe was throbbing. Rather than start all over, she thought, *fuck the coffee,* and putting cookies in a straw basket, brought it over, setting it on the cocktail table in front of him.

Barry helped himself to a cookie. He glanced at the table looking for a cup of coffee but was more engrossed in the news than his need, at that moment, for coffee. Mary sat on the couch.

When the news ended, he looked over at Mary, smiling, and told her what a pleasant time he was having. Mary smiled back. Other than her throbbing toe, and the grey chocolates, the spilled coffee, the broken cups, and Tucker Carlson, all was good with the world.

Yawning, Barry lifted himself out of the Barcalounger. Standing, he hoisted his jeans by his belt. They had slid below his belly. "Well, gotta call it a night. I have an early golf game tomorrow."

He started for the door with Mary following. At the door, he turned to her and noticed, for the first time, she still had a bump on her forehead where she had hit it on the dashboard when he stopped short. He saw the black and blue bruise, where her makeup was wearing off.

He also couldn't help but see that she was walking with a slight limp. *Gotta check to see if I was seein' right; that she has six toes.* Barry turned and gave Mary a hug and a cheek kiss. "We gotta do this again. Thank you for a fun evening."

With Barry on the other side of the door, Mary smiled to herself. The evening went well. He enjoyed her cooking and made himself at home. Even though the time they spent together was short, she felt they would see one another again.

Mary hobbled into the kitchen, sidestepping the shards of china and broken cookies, and proceeded to clean up from dinner. It was nice to have a man to cook and clean for. Then she changed the channel.

The Whining Chronicles

PART III

THIRTY-THREE

Why do I Live Here?

"Whining as an art form. You have a way of turning complaining into funny stories." Carey

We moved here when FLOML became disgruntled after five years in our previous condo. After moving more than twenty times, I lost track of the addresses we had. Like the plant of the same name, we epitomized the *Wandering Jew(s)*. He flew the coop shortly after we moved. My part in the partnership was earning money.

Being a realtor meant being on call 24/7/365. It was his responsibility to pay the bills and watch over our investments. In hindsight, I foolishly never paid close attention, nor did I learn how to run a household. I never paid a bill, being told early in the marriage, "If you're not going to pay them, don't open them." So, I didn't!

Now, leaving me high and dry, I had to do a quick study in paying bills and how to deal with the myriad of issues one must know when one is living alone in order to keep the lights burning and the a/c cooling.

The original windows in the almost forty-year-old building needed to be replaced. It was time to stop wedging those little Formica samples I borrowed from Home Depot between the frames and the windows to keep them from rattling in the breeze.

I ordered wind-resistant windows. The new windows, to quote my attorney, (more about that later) make my condo 'dark and dreary.' Someone fucked up. Mine are more darkly tinted than any of my neighbors'. Gloom enveloped my condo like a veil.

In 2011, Hollywood city officials determined anyone who lives close to or on the beach and replaces their windows must do so with *Turtle Gray* tinted ones. Right now, I am close to, but with global climate change may soon be, on the beach.

From March 1st through October 31st, turtles come onshore to lay their eggs. No, don't think Normandy Invasion. When they descend upon us; these guys just bob up, here and there. Not dissimilar to Sodom or Gomorrah and Lot's wife who would turn to shit[1] if she turned around upon leaving town.

Rumor has it, if the turtles see your light, they will turn into *Teenage Mutant Ninja Turtles* and climb, in my case, ten floors to lay their eggs. *No clear windows for you, m'lady!*

I chose my condo for its southern brightness and water views. Through my glass doors and windows, I can view, although somewhat dismally, both the Atlantic Ocean and the Intra-Coastal Waterway. My new sliding glass doors, which I was told by another attorney, after reviewing my contract's numerical description translated into *limo gray*.

I was supposed to get Turtle Gray which has a considerably lighter tint. My dark condo induces, *nap time;* anytime. If these windows were in my car, I would be cited for having the tint too dark for the police to see in.

Even when the sun is at its apex, from inside looking out, it looks like it's about to rain. It is constantly gray and dreary, not unlike what I imagine some of New Jersey is like. When I slide a door open, I am blinded by the light. I am in the midst of a legal dispute. Who is going to pay for replacement windows? If proven to be a factory fuck-up, the window company should replace them. Unfortunately, that thought involves logic, and as we all know, the law does not always involve logic.

The line from the song *Sleepy Time Gal*, 'you're turning night into day' spins around in my head, becoming a persistent and unwelcome mantra. Daytime naps do not make up for my sleepless nights.

I am sleep-deprived. I am bothered by a motorized vibration, a hum. For the past two months, I've tried ignoring the noise, my justification being the upstairs neighbor was renovating, had a de-humidifier, was on oxygen, or was drying out wall-to-wall carpeting. Either that or FPL has installed a power station in the condo above mine.

Turning my TV louder than the hum didn't work. Earplugs didn't either and forget listening to music, the hum seemed to get louder or my paranoia's getting the best of me, which is easy since I'm so worn out over this. I do manage to catch some *zzz's* during the day, lying on my couch looking out at the gloom.

Well, if I can't sleep why should my upstairs' neighbor? After more than two months of 24/7 noise, I reached my breaking point. At 6:45 a.m. I knocked on the door. No answer. After building up from a gentle knock to a pounding, a gentleman opened the door. I asked him to shut off his noisemaker. Lucky for me he was half asleep. He swore, politely, that he had no machinery, lifesaving or otherwise, and wished me luck in finding out what and where the hum was coming from. (He moved out two weeks later). The common hall A/C, that's it! That's what was making a racket.

I was dozing while leaning on the door of the building manager's office, waiting for it to open at 9 a.m. I almost fell in when the office manager's assistant pulled open the door from her side on her way to the mailbox. I prevailed on the manager to do something about the noise. He assured me he would. Fine. Now I'll go back to my condo and nap on the couch.

That night, tucked into bed, I heard *THAT* noise again. I went to the lobby and asked the security lady to summon the supervisor on call. Upon hearing the racket, he turned off the A/C on the tenth and eleventh floors. Quiet, at last! The sound of silence was deafening. Smiling to myself, I burrowed into my pillow waiting to be awash with peaceful sleep.

Wait! *THAT* noise! Two minutes on, ten seconds off and repeat. What the hell??? After tossing and turning, at 2 a.m. I went to investigate, taking the elevator from the tenth to the eleventh floor. The A/C was *dead as a doornail.* That same racket though was coming from the eleventh-floor unit's A/C that is in the hall closet opposite my unit, one floor up. Shit!

I called the snowbirds in New Jersey on Saturday. Yes, they were told by the manager of my (newest) complaint and assured me they would call their service company to do whatever is necessary. I was reassured the problem would be solved and tried to psych myself into not letting it get to me. It will be fixed.

Tired, but in a better mood, I convinced myself the noise and the windows will be taken care of...eventually. Although it appears to emanate from the floor above, sound carries through concrete, and like that pesky palmetto bug you know is lurking in the shadows, it takes fortitude to find the source. Be patient, I *mantra-ed* to myself.

"You're welcome." The hall and the snowbird's A/C's needed replacing anyways I was told, but hark, what do I hear? It sure ain't Santa and eight tiny reindeer. Late Sunday afternoon, listening at closed doors for sounds, I felt like Elmer Fudd hunting for that *scwewy wabbit.*

Maybe a long walk on the *Hollywood Broadwalk* will calm me. Looks like it's gonna rain, though. I went anyways; it didn't rain. There was not a storm cloud in the blue sky. Damn those windows.

Wanting a snack before heading out I headed for my kitchen. Oh! No! My kitchen counter was bugged; overrun with Zettabytes, the tiniest of bugs one can hardly see with the naked eye. Being not of sound mind I stood there watching them. They're so teeny. Hmmm, do they have hearts and lungs? Where do they come from and where do they rest when they get tired of scurrying around and snacking on my crackers? Do they ever look at one another and ask, "Do I look fat?" *Don't overthink the life of the not much larger than no-see-ums; the do-see-ums,* I cautioned myself. I *Raid*-i-ated them. *Now I have earned the title of the (ex)terminator,* I snickered to my sleep-deprived self.

One night, at my wit's end, I needed someone to bear witness to the incessant, intermittent two-minute hummm followed by ten seconds of silence which sounds louder at 3 a.m. than 3 p.m. I called security and asked for the person in charge to come to my unit. Until another human heard what I heard I was losing my credibility as being (reasonably) normal and not just a dotty old lady who hears noises.

He arrived dressed in his short-sleeved blue uniform and a cap with *Kent Security* stitched on it. "Hi, I'm Butch," said the brawny young man with many tattoos covering his burly arms. The one that caught my eye was the assault weapon inked on his forearm. Knowing why he was there, he apologized as I opened the door. "My hearing isn't too good," he said.

Probably blew out his eardrums firing assault weapons I guessed. He took one step in, stopped in his tracks, and said, "Boy, that noise is annoying!." Finally! my paranoia was validated.

We walked around my condo, listening. He claimed that he could hear the ceaseless noise even in the closets and outside in the common hallway. He offered to listen at other doors to find the cause. He assured me he would write up what he heard and give it to Bruce, one of the two chief engineers when he got to work at 8 a.m.

At 10 a.m. I went to the office to see David, the building manager. "Did you get the report from Bruce?" I asked.

"Bruce is off on Tuesdays."

"Did Butch leave a report for you? I queried.

"Who's Butch?" After dousing me with ice water to revive me, David assured me Bruce would come to see me the next day. His sleuthing found the sound was coming from old water pipes. Temporarily fixed, until the new pipes are installed, I regale the delicious thought of the sound of silence in my future.

---

1. That may be salt. Check your local bible.

THIRTY-FOUR

Sex-a-peel

C ould I have been prepping for annus horribilis 2020 for the past five years and not known it?

"Now that you've retired from a career in real estate, what do you do to keep busy?" My friends and inquiring minds persistently asked this question following my permanent hiatus from work and after being *on call* seven days a week for almost forty-five years. My answer to them was, "Define busy." One can be "busy" whether they are doing something...or nothing. It took a pandemic for others to learn that after being at home, day after day after day, everyone's characterization of "busy" is not the same.

In my fantasy world, I' lounge on my divan, watching commercial-free movies, crunching on chips, popcorn, or enjoying the soothing and refreshing company of Ben and Jerry. I never gain an ounce, being blessed with a rapid, yet very healthy thyroid, and low cholesterol.

In a previous chapter, *Why Do I Live Here?* I wrote about my new heavily tinted windows. This is the continuing saga of my bleak house, in deference to C. Dickens' 1852 best seller, *Bleak House*.

Looking every bit like the evil Miss Hannigan, the owner of the orphanage where *Annie's* folks dropped her off as a small child, the representative from the manufacturer of the windows, showed up at my door alongside the owner of the company who installed the dark dismal windows. They both sported cold, sour, and dour faces. From their expressions and demeanor, one would think they had each just missed winning the lotto by one number.

I greeted them as warmly as any dissatisfied customer could. After cool introductions were exchanged, they studied the windows, muttering to each other, while taking cell phone pics. I asked if they needed more light to take their pictures, but they merely scowled in recognition of my point.

When I ordered my windows, I had no reason to assume I wouldn't be getting the same tint as others installed in other units by this same company in my condo building. The tint is required by the city of Hollywood due to the city's concern that turtles coming out of the ocean to lay their eggs were getting confused by residents' lighting and could very possibly lose their way back into the waves and mistake my dimly lit living room for the Atlantic Ocean.

Miss Hannigan and the contractor mumbled something about getting back to me, but not saying when. I was going to regale them with my "turtles in the living room" story but decided for the better.

Meanwhile, life marched on, and with it, trials and tribulations. My garbage disposal had shorted out the week before and a replacement was being installed. Miguel showed up two hours after the *guaranteed* appointment time, which is pretty much right on time for South Florida. He pulled out the cleaning supplies drawer under the sink, left to go to his truck for piping material, returned, made a phone call, and then explained to me he was unable to replace the dead disposal.

It seemed that my new sink, installed five months before, was deeper than the one that was replaced and didn't leave enough vertical spacing for a new drainpipe and disposal. Miguel put the drawer back on its tracks, tried shoving it in, and made a hasty retreat.

"Wait!" I called out as I ran out the door just in time to see the elevator doors slide closed. My cupboard door did not close. It looked like a gaping tooth in my otherwise tidy kitchen. I realized then that possibly the only positive thing about this debacle was the view.

I tried pushing the drawer back into place but with no luck. I had to leave soon for appointments so I thought, *I'll deal with this later.* That evening, rushing home, with minutes to spare to freshen up for my date I tried closing the cupboard door, but the drawer was stuck. Damn! *I'll deal with this tomorrow.*

Four days prior, I had visited *Facial Xpressions* for a consultation. At my age, trying to hold back the aging process is akin to holding back a tidal wave with outstretched arms.

Lori, the esthetician, convinced me to, "Have a chemical peel." Fast, easy, and *can you believe my luck!* on sale for the month of September. Had I been there in October, I have no doubt it would have been on sale for the month of October.

She speed-read the details of how it would work and the amazing results I could expect. *Hmmm, will I be more appealing* after this peeling I wondered? She coated my face with something wet that smelled like a decomposing raccoon.

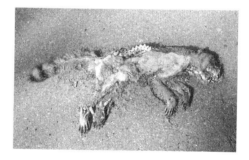

After taking my money she told me how to care for the *treated area*, aka my face. Not too bad; some tingling, some redness, and then some peeling. I was to follow her directions, which I requested she write down in detail, not wanting to rely on my declining memory.

By day three I looked as though I had fallen asleep under a sun lamp, looking like a red-hot mama. By the end of the day, my face was feeling tight, tingling and I looked like the last prune in the bowl in the dining room of an assisted living facility. It began itching as I started molting.

On day four, I called Lori per her instructions. She told me what I shouldn't have done; put a moisturizer on, especially on my cheeks which had not yet begun to peel.

"Why didn't you tell me that?" I implored her, as I had diligently followed her instructions.

"No harm, no foul, the solution will do its thing, but it will take longer than the original wait of three or four days," she glibly responded.

Holy cow! Trying not to scratch my very itchy skin, I did a double-take when I looked in the mirror. The dry skin was hanging all over my chin, forehead, and nose like flesh-colored icicles hanging from a gutter on an early thaw day in February. I carefully trimmed the hangers-on with scissors. I looked like something from a low-budget horror movie.

Shit! He's here. I didn't want to scare my gentleman caller off so at the *ding* of my doorbell I grabbed my house keys, opening the door at the *dong*, and brushed by him with nary a nod. He dutifully followed me to the elevator.

I live at the south end of the *Hollywood Broadwalk,* where the outdoor lighting is almost nonexistent. Perfect. Stan is a slow walker which I usually find vexing but tonight it suited me jussst fine. "Let's rest" I conciliatorily offered after three minutes of slow strolling, and still in the dark. "Why don't we sit here." *He swallowed the Kool-Aid.*

Strolling, slowly back to my condo after what seemed like acceptable chatting time, we walked to his car which, fortuitously was not parked under a streetlight. He was expecting an invite back to my condo for, at least a glass of water, since he drove from Boca Raton, but yawning, I bade him goodnight, with my head slightly askew. I couldn't wait to get home and ease the itching by *gently* rubbing the sloughing skin off my molting face.

On day five, after an itchy and scratchy restless sleep, I wanted to tackle the protruding kitchen drawer. Taking everything out of it I saw that the back of the frame of the drawer had come apart. Not handy with tools I resorted to good ol' crazy glue.

Shit! Two of my fingers fused together. That did not stop me from the task at hand. I squeezed the corners together with my eight remaining digits until it, like my fingers, bonded together. Having remembered *the fix* from having been stuck on myself many years ago, I didn't panic.

I checked with Google, and, yes, nail polish remover was still an acceptable treatment for reclaiming your fingers without ripping the skin off, and, best of all, my cupboard door now closed. Adding to my angst of the dark windows, I now have no garbage disposal, and I would do anything to scratch my flaking face. Boy, after this peeling I better be verrry appealing.

Now what! Those fuckin' bugs are back. Don't know why they're called *noseeums*; I do *seeum*. Unlike ants, whose colonies seem to have structure, these guys scurry around helter-skelter on my kitchen counter. I wonder if they know they can now breathe a sigh of relief. The threat of being wiped up and ground up in the disposal is gone.

I must admit, things are in balance. No disposal, but yes on insect intrusions. No on any filtered light into my home, but yes on a kitchen drawer that closes. No on a great date, but yes on a flaking face…see, life appears to balance out.

Trying to get my mind off my itchy face I fixate on the life of the I-seeums. Perhaps I'll build them a tiny playground with a seesaw and an obstacle course. They can race one another. I'll be the judge. Do they respond to music? As far as pets go, they're certainly easier to take care of than, say, a gerbil. When I leave for the day, do they pine away, waiting for my return? I think not. They seem to be very independent and appear to be here to stay.

That afternoon a call from one of my "I'll do you a favor for a fee", attorneys called to report that Ms. Hannigan and Ben said that I should have known the windows would be darker and they are not replacing them for less than an additional $10,000. She informed me that she does not have the expertise to go further, and I must now find a *construction defect* lawyer.

Not so fast. "For an additional fee, please send one more letter," I implored her and told her what to write. Meanwhile, I watch the *I-see-ums* scuttling around my bananas while I ponder, *what DO I do to keep busy?*

THIRTY-FIVE

Memories
_____

There's no such thing as a quick fix when it comes to trying to put the brakes on how you look while careening to the finish line. I had a procedure called Platelet Rich Plasma (PRP). This procedure uses your own tissue, which in simple layman's terms, is done by drawing blood from your vein and injecting it back into your face. It is a pre-cursor to a stem cell procedure that one day may work. The day after the procedure, my face became red, white, black, and blue. It looked as though I attempted to stop a slamming door with my face.

PRP has been shown to improve skin texture, smoothing out crepey skin and wrinkles. The results will be visible in four to six weeks, so says the pamphlet with the smiling twenty-something model, with the perfect complexation, on the cover. As if she might ever need PRP in the next thirty years. In six weeks, the esthetician will either be pleased to see me and the results, or when I get there, she may no longer be in business. We'll see.

Reclining on my couch, watching TV, was akin to watching a three-ring circus. The president's choice for a Supreme Court Justice is having his credentials scrutinized and many in the news media are falling over themselves painting as lurid a picture as possible, trying him in the court of public opinion.

Waiting for my gentleman caller in my dark, dreary, condo, with my dead garbage disposal and my live *I-see-ums*, I flipped through the channels and began ruminating about my life as a young child.

I consider myself to be an honest person… now. Not Supreme Court Justice honest, but as honest as one can be, who doesn't claim to have a squeaky-clean background and is not up for a lifetime job. If I was nominated, an FBI scrutiny background check might reveal my life of crime. Not a, *something to keep me up at night* problem though. Not to worry, no one's knocking down my door offering me that appointment. Thinking back, I can't remember any Supreme Court Justices having a prior job as a real estate agent.

Growing up in West Hartford in the 1950s, the label *latch-key kid* didn't exist. Nobody I knew used keys or latches to secure their homes. "The back door is open" or, "The key is under the mat" was about as much security as we had.

My elementary school was at the end of my block. Walking home for lunch every day was an easy hop, skip, and a jump, to an empty home and a warm meal sitting on a still-warm stove.

My mother cleaned our home, or, as she described it, "straightened up" and left supper on the stove, leaving the cooling meal for me to dip into for my lunch. Then, dressed in business-like clothes, with nylon stockings held up by the garters on her girdle, she rushed off, to "catch the bus." As a little girl, my mind was awash with the image of this old lady; Mom was about thirty-five at the time, running down the center of the road in her high heels chasing the bus until she was able to 'catch it' to get to her job as a keypunch operator at the Aetna Life Insurance Company.

My father got dressed every day in a three-piece suit, tie, and hat, and drove to his accounts in his new celadon green Studebaker. He sold liquor to the *package stores,* as the liquor stores are called in Connecticut. Occasionally he found a friendly game of *Pinochle* he couldn't pass up.

Sometimes my lunch was meatballs and sauce which, was ladled over spaghetti for our supper that evening, or chicken or beef marinating. As tasty as it was, after I ate, I was never satisfied. There was never anything sweet for dessert. To me, dessert is akin to the dot that marks the end of a sentence. To this day I must have a sweet. Preferably chocolate. It tells my brain, "Your meal is over. You're finished *chubbo.*"

Three blocks from home, was the Kingswood Market, our neighborhood food store in an English Tudor-style two-storied building. To save time, during the last half hour of my hour-long lunchtime, I rode my red Columbia two-wheeler there.

Some things never change. Then, as now, candy bars were displayed at the front of the store, under the cash register. Every school day I went there, having no change of my own, and, unbeknownst to the shopkeeper, helped myself to candy. By the time I retired from my life of petty crime I had eaten and knew every candy bar in the store. I wonder if exposing my days of crime will come back to bite me in my old age.

My stealing spree ended when I was twelve and started baby-sitting. With my first earnings, I walked a mile to a donut store in the West Hartford Center, which is what we called downtown West Hartford. I learned what a baker's dozen was. It's thirteen donuts for the price of twelve. Boy, that was my lucky day. I sauntered back home eating all thirteen donuts, enjoying the fruits of my labor.

So engrossed was I in reliving this old memory that was stored in the recesses of my brain, I almost didn't hear the doorbell, "Are you still molting?" Stan asked as he started to step into my dark condo. *And I thought he hadn't noticed my face last week when I was so careful to stay in the shadows.* Lit only by the table lamp at the far end of my living room, the room was dim.

He tripped over the threshold and fell into my arms. I gave him a quick hug, avoiding a face-to-face greeting, and hustled him off to the movies. I caught him staring at me in the darkened theater when I sneaked a peek. At this time in our blooming relationship, he didn't know what I looked like and neither did I. After the movie I drove back to my condo and dropped him off at his car which was parked in front of the building.

"Call me when you're finished," he said simply, as we exchanged goodnights. He slid out of my car, got into his, and drove off. Five more weeks to see if my face fix worked…and if there is a Stan in my future. Like settling the issue of my dark windows, only time will tell.

THIRTY-SIX

Mecca Market

S tan never met a thrift shop or flea market he didn't like, or for that matter ever drove by one without stopping. The *Festival Flea Market* in Pompano and the *Swap Shop* in Ft. Lauderdale are two of his favorite haunts, and in deference to Stan, he does find a lot of treasures, depending, of course on one's definition of 'treasure'. But how many treasures does one person need? He has thirty pairs of reading glasses and can never find even one when he needs them. At last count, he has at least seven computers. I think, you only need one of any one thing, other than socks, underwear, or certain body parts. Multiple items have a way, like magic, of disappearing when you need them. One of something has a home of its own, like your toothbrush; but you need to leave it in the same place.

When he's not shopping in thrift shops, he toils at flea markets. He owns a home in Monticello, New York, and he's there for every legal holiday in the summer and fall to work the huge outdoor markets that attract hundreds of thousands of people who can't resist a bargain or the opportunity to discover their own hidden treasures. He is not a seller of seashells by the seashore, but a bag man, verging dangerously close to being classified as a hoarder.

He sells disposable bags for vacuum cleaners and has a collection of thousands of bags for every brand of vacuum manufactured since 1960. Owning more than a hundred and fifty vacuum cleaners, he is the *go-to* guy to buy one if you want one that is old, clunky, noisy, and hard to push. (Hmm, that *sort of describes some of the men I know.*) He even has one of the *Flintstone* models, that he claims is the "top of the line."

One Saturday afternoon Stan called, all excited. He bought me a surprise. He is an *app man,* having an app on his phone alerting him to flea markets and tag sales in Broward and Palm Beach Counties. Today it was a flea market, and lo and behold, it was only five miles from his home. He was certain I didn't have what he bought. *Whatever the surprise, more than likely I already have one, don't need one or don't want one,* I woefully thought.

Oh, well, put on a smile I said to myself while scrutinizing my face in my magnifying mirror. I see no youthful-looking improvements from having the facial procedures several weeks ago. The slow healing black and blue marks from the injection sites have turned a yellowish green...a color that you will not find in a super-sized box of Crayola's or even on paint sample cards in Home Depot.

Stan showed up at my condo with a huge grin on his face, like a clown with a banjo, carrying a wrinkled Publix bag in his hand. He was holding his latest perceived treasure.

"Here", he said, as he unceremoniously handed me the bag with his newly acquired bounty. Pulling out an odd black garment, I didn't have a clue as to what it was. Holding it up, not knowing if it was right side up, or inside out, one thing was for certain, I didn't already have one, need one, or want one, whatever this *one* was.

"I give up" I said as I held it first one way and then another. "What is it?"

"It's a *Bushiyya*."

Wait a minute! It looks like something ladies on the news from the Persian Gulf wear. "A what?" I croaked.

"The woman who sold it to me showed me what to do. Taking it from my hands he explained, "It's a veil that you tie onto your forehead, and it drapes over your entire face." Curious, I took it from him, holding it up to my face, not knowing which end was up.

"How do you wear it? It has no slits for the eyes."

"No," Stan explained, as I handed it back to him. "You don't need them; the fabric is sheer enough to see through."

Hmm, sort of like the Chinese tour bus, I thought.

"Now you and I don't have to lurk in the shadows waiting for your face to finish peeling."

Yea, right, like I'm ever gonna wear this. Guess he was too excited about his new treasure to notice my face had almost healed. Don't look a gift horse in the mouth, I was taught early on in life. If someone is nice enough to think of you and buy you a gift, be gracious and say, "Thank you."

"Thank you" I said out loud while thinking, *There is less chance of me wearing this than wearing Lady Gaga's meat dress.*

God knows I tried, I really tried, but I couldn't get the words out. Stan helped me secure it to my forehead. He tied it at the back of my head and let it fall, covering my face and shoulders. "I'm gettin' hot!" As I was being shrouded, beads of sweat broke out on my upper torso and I suddenly had this strange urge to rob a bank.

"What's it made of?" I heard myself ask from under the veil, already knowing the answer.

He replied, "Polyester."

"Remember what I told you once before when you wanted to buy me a caftan? I can't wear polyester. It makes me sweat. It doesn't breathe and neither can I." I reproached him as gently as possible, relieved I didn't have to make any other excuses.

"Oh right! Now I remember," Stan declared.

"Darn," I said, pulling the black shroud off and gasping for air. The message I was attempting to convey was the *If only* one. *If only* it wasn't polyester, I would have jumped for joy, gleefully acknowledging his thoughtfulness, wearing it in public just long enough to be denied boarding a plane. "I'll be happy to pay for it." I lied.

"Nah, that's ok. I'll let you pay for dinner." He said, with a twinkle in his eye.

"Well, how much was it?" I queried, wondering if this meant dining in a restaurant or Wendy's drive-through?

Hesitating, he sheepishly confessed, "It was fifty cents."

Oh good, we're off to the sno-cone store for dinner. I stifled my curiosity and didn't ask what else this nice Jewish guy couldn't resist buying. He later told me it was a *one-day-only* flea market in the basement of the Islamic Center Mosque in Pompano. Meanwhile, he's staring at me, as if seeing me for the first time, seeing me with the lights on in my otherwise dark condo.

I am asking myself, *what does a nice Jewish girl do with a shmatteh[1] designed to cover up the person inside.* Not to worry, I'm sure in my free time, I'll think of something. Hmmm, Halloween is around the corner.

---

1. A worthless rag.

THIRTY-SEVEN

The Eyes Have It

I wanted to see better. My right eye was covered by my hooded eyelid. Think of my lids as matching window shades. One pulled down three-quarters of the way and the other down only one quarter, with varying percentages of each brown eye peering out from under them. Now you get the picture.

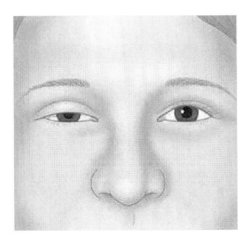

At times, especially at the end of the day, my droopy eyelids, especially the right one, looked like a turtle's. My eyesight was affected and the droopier they got, the less I saw.

I thought, before they drooped anymore, leaving me completely in the dark, I would have them, like tiebacks for drapes, tacked up. I had a condition known as *Ptosis*, also referred to as droopy eyelids. The standard surgical procedure consists of a surgeon lifting the lid's muscle and re-attaching it to the eyelid. It is then held together with a stitch in the crease of the eyelid.

The five different eye doctors I went to all agreed that after having this procedure, I should be able to see street signs for the streets from a reasonable distance, eliminating that bothersome and dangerous sudden stop and swerve onto the street I was seeking. I don't want to have to put some type of warning sign in my rear window.

I scheduled my surgery. Debby, my doctor's assistant, gave me an info book called the *Surgery Center.* On the first page it reads, *you will be contacted by someone from the center two days before surgery to go over the procedure.* When was the last time you called a doctor or a medical center and left a message? How long did you have to wait until they called back? Or did they call back? The order of the day seems to be, *you call me; I don't call you.* I found out that most medical schools teach this method of communication so as not to bother doctors with trivial calls from frantic patients.

Two days before surgery I heard nothing. The following day, the day before *D Day*, the info book declared, *The Surgery Center hours start at 6 a.m.* At 6:45 I called and was upbraided by a voice announcing *if you are calling about a pre-or post-surgical procedure you will be called.* Click. I was unceremoniously disconnected.

I called again after nine. On my third attempt to be connected to the voice of a warm-blooded person, I pressed the prompt that said, *"If you are a doctor or calling from a doctor's office, please press one."* I thought about that for two seconds remembering that I did work as a medical assistant in the 1970's for a year so I pressed one. A lovely lady who apologized for answering the phone on the twentieth ring, told me, "Leave your number, I will call you back," and I should, "Have a blessed day."

Seeds of doubt began to pop through the soil that I would need more than blessings if I was going to get through this day stress-free. I called my surgeon's office at 9:15 and was informed, via a recorded voice that, "If this is an emergency hang up and call 911." It was the same message as the surgery center's *press two* prompt. I did not receive a callback, nor did I call 911 although the thought to call 911 and report them did cross my mind.

Staying calm and using my Sunday best nice voice, I left a message asking Dr. Singer, my surgeon, to call me back ASAP. I wasn't certain how long I would need for convalescing and wanted to go food shopping. At 10:15 I called the doctor's office and asked for Debby, who I knew from when I had cosmetic surgery almost twenty years before; an attractive lady in her mid-fifties, very efficient, very pleasant, and very nice. Or was she…

"Oh," the receptionist said blithely, "She just went into an examining room with the doctor and a patient. But of course, she will call you as soon as she gets out." *Of course, she will!*

After waiting two hours I called back. Debby was unavailable. I insisted she return my call. Now, the *keep calm and carry-on* tee-shirts people wear were beginning to make sense to me. Keeping my cool was beginning to thaw and was now at the lukewarm stage.

My plans to meet friends at noon fell by the wayside since it was now 12:15. The receptionist, hardly able to conceal her annoyance, answered my concerns demanding, "What is the problem? You will be called!" I explained I wanted to get on with my day, as well as stock up on groceries since I might be homebound 'anywhere from two days to two weeks.'

Ms. Snarky snapped, "You are not the only one. Everyone is busy."

At this point, there was only one person I cared about, and it was *moi*. I implored her to call the Surgery Center, telling her I had left messages including one on the doctors' line with no results. "I don't have time to do this", she spat into the phone, "I will be breaking protocol." *Who gives a shit about protocol?* I wanted to snap back.

"I am very busy. This is not my job" and with a heavy disgusted sigh reluctantly resigned that she would make the call. She repeated herself as if I didn't hear her the first time.

Not more than two minutes after hanging up with Debby I received a call from Maria, from the Surgery Center. I answered endless questions about my and my parent's health. Whoa! Was I having a heart transplant or a lid lift? No, she did not know what time my procedure would be but, regardless, I needed to be at the Center at 7:30 a.m. She told me no drinking or eating past 11:59 tonight.

I explained if I go without eating or drinking for an extended period, my blood sugar drops and I fall into what I call my *deficit spending*, some of the symptoms being confusion, shakiness, and anxiety. *Yeah, right, like she was hearing that for the first time!*

She allowed that I could have certain juices up until 5:59 a.m. the day of the procedure. That relieved me of that anxiety but by now I wondered if my blood pressure was through the ceiling from all this unnecessary stress.

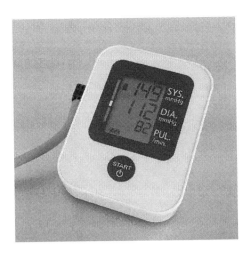

Later that evening my designated driver #1 called to say she was not well enough to drive me to the Center. I called the backup. "Oh, geez, I can take you, but I won't be able to pick you up." Great! Now what? Just as I was wondering who to call, a neighbor called to ask if she could do anything for me. Yup! What a relief. We confirmed a 6:50 a.m. pick up and she would retrieve me about noon. All good.

D-Day. Ensconced in one of six cubicles in the holding area, comfy in my just out of the warming oven blankets, I overheard that Dr. Singer was stuck behind a traffic collision on I-95 and would be late. By now I was on an IV drip to keep me hydrated, keeping my sugar level steady and it was dripping some relaxant stuff in for good measure. Wonder if they sell this stuff at Walgreens?

Dr. Singer arrived and told me I was number two; my wait would be about forty-five minutes. Well, nothing to do but watch the hustle and bustle of the medical staff move around. They all looked like they were about to walk out at any minute, and I am positive it was not to make any return phone calls. It was somewhat disconcerting that they were bundled up in winter jackets. I guess it's easier to freeze germs than rely on them to be disinfected by hospital cleaners.

My turn came and I was wheeled into the OR and greeted by Debby and the Doc. The next thing I remember was being coerced with apple juice and cookies as my incentive to wake up. They literally threw my clothes on me and ushered me out the door. Ok, *ushered* might not be the exact right word.

Later, I was told each doctor was allotted only so much time for each victim, err, patient so I guess my meter had expired.

I returned home none the worse. Although the instructions were specific that someone was supposed to be with me at home, I managed just fine on my own. I was instructed to buy two post-procedure prescriptions that I needed to start that night and repeat twice a day. One, a Vaseline-like salve stated in capital letters, *FOR EACH EYE.* The other eyedrops, were a no-brainer. The salve, in the eyes or, if not in them, then where? I put a dab inside my bottom lids and after blinking couldn't see through the greasy residue. It was like being underwater without a mask. Oh well, I was seeing the doctor the next day. After repeating the procedure, the next morning, blurry eyed, I was driven to the doctor. It was as if I was riding a tour bus through China in a smog-laden haze.

I asked Debby where I was supposed to apply the salve. "I'll let you know." She must have said this with her fingers crossed behind her back. I left with no answer. I continued to put a dab on my bottom lids and greasing up my vision.

On Monday I called and asked to speak to her. Repeating my question and asking how long I needed to use it, I mentioned my appointment for the coming Friday.

"Why are you coming?" she demanded.

"To take the stitches out."

"You didn't have any," she snapped.

Guess she forgot that I saw her in the OR and the day after in the office. Repeating my question as to how the salve was to be used, she told me, "Read the label!"

"I did. It said, *use as directed*." She told me to only use it at night and put it inside the eyes. I asked why I wasn't given specific directions.

After a few seconds, she snorted, "Could've, should've, would've? What's the problem?"

Only my eyes, you fuck-head! I was told to 'take it easy for a few days. *Take it easy? For a few days?* 'Use as directed', what exactly do they all mean? Oh yes, I was also told, 'don't bend over (and? or?) pick up anything heavier than fifty pounds.' *Don't bend over? Oh no, and I was planning on going to a strawberry U-pick farm today...damn.*

After a week, I went for a swim in the pool which, upon asking, was told not to because "The pool is dirty." I don't know how this doctor knew my pool, but I made certain to keep my head above water and didn't do anything strenuously athletic, which was no problem since nothing *strenuously athletic* has ever been part of my daily regimen, dating back to...forever.

Thirteen days later, cabin fever enveloped me, and I decided to go ballroom dancing. I would tread lightly aware of my freshly attached lids. I was asked to dance by Arthur who told me he danced more like Fred, Astaire that is, than Arthur Murray. He was right, he did dance like Fred, but much to Arthur's chagrin, I was still not allowed to bend over and no dipping. Not even coming close to dancing like Fred's longtime partner Ginger Rogers, the only thing she and I had in common was that we both danced backward.

Then there was John, a good dancer who didn't speak English and danced, cheek to cheek while nibbling on my ear. I was a little uneasy since it was less than two weeks since I had the eye job and mindful of the fact that I was told to not bend over nor do anything strenuous for a few weeks. I am still amazed by the fact that not doing anything strenuous would cause me so much angst and missed opportunities.

While dancing I thought if I tilt my head down will my eyeballs fall out? Should I explain to Fred or John, the cheek-to-cheek guy, that I recently had my eyeballs stitched to my eyelids? Wouldn't that be better than spooking them out by crying, "Hey, I have my eye on you," and mean it when it plops onto their shoulder?

Can you picture eighty-year-old plus folks crawling around on their hands and knees, assuming they could get down on their hands and knees, looking for somebody's balls, eyeballs that is? All's well that ends well. My eyes and lids are a matched set and they're still in my head. Reading street signs, not so good. After the dance, John asked if we could see each other again. I told him, "I'll see."

The procedure was covered by Medicare and Blue Cross. The surgeon's staff tried convincing me to use his private facilities for the procedure which would not have been covered by insurance and to have some cosmetic eye lifting while I was having what was necessary and insured. By declining I am convinced that is why the plastic surgeon and his assistants abused their responsibilities, as well as me, by not even trying to hide their disdain.

When I had cosmetic surgery, which was not covered by insurance eighteen years previous, the red carpet was rolled out for me. My cost at that time, although I don't remember exactly, was more than $10,000. Shame on these same personnel to show their true colors.

In the middle of the afternoon on a Tuesday I listened to a recording: "You have reached the offices of Doctors Meekle, Deakle, Drek, Schneider, and Tompkins. No one is available to take your call right now. If this is an emergency, please call 911 or go directly to your emergency room. Thank you for calling." Click!

During regular hours 9 to 5 Monday through Friday, is it wrong to expect a doctor's office to answer? Speaking your name and number to a mechanical device is no guarantee of a call-back.

The doctor will eventually see you in the hospital. By the time he shows up, you have had multiple tests and your hospital bill may rival the cost of a Lamborghini. Doctors can charge more since they are seeing us in the hospital. How do we change it? Or would that be as difficult as it would be to persuade the NRA to eliminate assault weapons?

THIRTY-EIGHT

Stan's Sleepover

Stan and I live fifty miles apart. We enjoy each other's company and he's fun to be with, but the long-distance makes it difficult to develop a close and more intimate relationship, creating what I refer to as "geographic incompatibility." My heart doesn't go pitter-patter at the sound of his name, nor at the thought of anything more intimate than sharing a Kit-Kat bar. When he is out of sight, he's out of mind. I do like him though, as a platonic friend.

On his evening visits to me, it's if too late for him to drive home, we sleep together, but not in the biblical sense. One of my house rules, which he agreed to, was that he stay on 'his' side of my queen-sized bed. To be assured that he accepted these rules and not wanting to disturb him in case his arm or a leg should breach our agreement, one night I devised a plan to avoid his possible wandering appendages before he 'accidentally' wandered onto my self-determined side. I thought of stopping in at the local Amish supply store and purchasing a bundling board, but alas and alack, no Amish stores nearby.

While Stan was in a deep sleep, I noiselessly slipped out of bed and like the proverbial church mouse, searched in my linen closet for the twin-sized sheets left over from the condo's previous owner. Making Chihuahua ear-sized loops at the corners with twine from my trusty old toolbox, I doubled it up, hooking the first loop over one of the large rusty nails I found in my kitchen junk drawer.

Spotting his hearing aids on the nightstand, I knew the noise wouldn't disturb him. I hammered the first nail into the wall above the bed. With my yardstick, I found the center of the bed, which was in the middle of the room, climbed on my two-step -folding ladder and struggled to secure the twine to the ceiling fan which I had turned off. I draped the used-to-be white, and now ol' yeller sheet with scenes of cute baby penguins wearing ski caps and scarfs skating on ponds, down the center of the bed.

Wait a second, sister, why not divide the entire room? I took the sheet down and stapled it to another pre-owned one. This one was faded blue with flying Supermen punching people with *POW* emblazoned across the space between his fists and the villains' faces.

At 2:30 a.m. in the blackness, I could make out Stan's body. Covered with fuzzy white body hair, he looked every bit like Mary's little lamb. He was lying on his side with his back to me. As I finished draping the sheets over the now sagging twine, he turned over. Still sound asleep, he caught the bottom corner of the Superman sheet where it met the penguins, taking both sheets with him as he curled up in a fetal position. The twine pulled out of the wall and the sheet sailed down over Stan. More asleep than awake, he panicked and started thrashing about. The more he flailed, the more entangled he became.

"If you stop thrashing, I'll get you untangled. It's ok, you're with me." I knew my words were falling on deaf ears when I spied his hearing aids still resting on the nightstand. He continued thrashing, entwining himself further amongst the sheets.

He slept on, but now in a snarled web of skating penguins, Superman, twine, and two rusty nails. He raised his arm, stretching it, and as he tucked it back to his chest, he caught the edge of the sheet that had settled on top of my high antique soda bottle table lamp. It began swaying from the weight, further entangling him.

Whew! That was close. I jumped off the ladder and was able to catch the lamp as it started its free-fall, but not without first seeing stars when I slammed my toes into the corner of the bed. Ooowwie!

Oh no! Just then, the TV roared to life with the World War II carpet bombing of Dresden and the Battle of Iwo Jima, which I'm sure my neighbors appreciated, being that I sleep with the sliding glass door open.

Stan slept on; unaware he had rolled over onto the remote which was under my pillow. My heart pounded in my head from the Dresden bombing and my elevated blood pressure. What the hell! He slept like a baby, drooling, not on his, but on my pillow. He had breached the terms of our agreement; he was completely on my side of the bed.

As I gathered up the sheets and twine, rolling them into a big ball, I stabbed myself in the palm of my hand with a rusty nail. Shit! Tossing the jumbled mess onto the floor of my closet, I went into the bathroom to clean the wound with hydrogen peroxide. Even with applied pressure, I couldn't stop the bleeding.

Finding some long-forgotten gauze in the medicine cabinet, probably left by the previous owners who left the sheets, I wrapped my hand in it and proceeded to remove any evidence of the night's activities.

Exhausted, I dragged myself into the living room and crashed on the couch. At dawn's early light Stan called out in his sing-song way, "Where are you my sweet? I had a good night sleep I hope you did too, except I had the craziest dream."

"Oh really, what was it?" I asked as I hobbled back to the bedroom, waiting for him to replay the night of horrors.

Before he had a chance to tell me, as he stretched the sleep out of himself, he hesitated. Looking towards the ceiling he spotted the hole in the wall over the bed.

"What happened?" He asked, plugging in his hearing aids. "I didn't notice that before we went to bed."

"You're very observant" I uttered, almost under my breath.

"Get under the covers, we'll snuggle" he tittered. As I started towards the bed he commented on my limping.

He asked, "What happened to your hand? Is that blood I see?"

"Oh, I caught my hand on something that was hanging around," I said.

"Did you sleep well, my little chickadee" he chortled as he turned down the comforter for me.

"Well, to be perfectly frank, you breached our agreement and slept on my side of the bed," I said as calmly as I could, through gritted teeth.

He looked crestfallen for a second, then his face lit up. Stan, who prides himself for being A Mr. Fix-it exclaimed, "How about I devise a divider? You know, sort of a faux bundling board. I'll make one. I'm pretty handy you know. Do you have a couple of twin-sized sheets and some rope? I'll sew the sheets together and put a molly screw in the hole in the wall so there won't be a need to make another one and screw one into the opposite wall. Then I'll drape the sheets over the clothesline for when I stay over." He then said with a big smile. "You know, sometimes I amaze myself with my amazing ideas. By the way, that crazy dream? I felt like I had returned to the womb."

Why Do I Travel?

PART IV

THIRTY-NINE

Dear Vincent

 On a visit to the South of France an evening walk on the grounds of the Saint-Paul Asylum in Saint-Remy-de-Provence turned out to be a spiritual experience.

Strolling, at 8 pm, the sun was still shining softly from the sky you painted, lighting the leaves of the trees you captured for all eternity.

The quiet crunch I heard, from the soft leaf -strewn earth softly giving way underfoot, was of my own making.

Beneath the canopies of the gnarled ancient olive trees the only other sound was the silence of your presence as I walked slowly through the canvas of your soul, with you by my side.

I write this as though it was only yesterday when you touched me, so many years ago.

The essence of that picture-perfect evening still moves me in a way nothing else does.

In April, my granddaughter Abbey and I will be visiting the Netherlands, your birthplace. I am anticipating you may, in some way, awake your spirit that has become part of me and when I least expect it, your presence will become known.

Until then, I remain reverential to your impact on me and your influence upon the world.

Brenda

FORTY

The Reality of Aging

Nobody wants to admit it or accept the fact that they are getting old. I don't either. I cannot believe the age I am, as Father Time keeps relentlessly moving on. Is there ever going to be an end of time, or is time timeless?

Sometimes when I look at myself, I see a younger woman who belies my chronological age. Other times, well, forget it.

The one thing we all share is that we love life. We will do everything and anything to make ourselves look better, feel better, and be better. One suggestion I offered in my primer, *Divorced After 56 years, Why am I Soo Happy?* was to find something near and dear to you and offer to volunteer.

I did just that. I signed on with SAR EL, an organization that refers volunteers to Israeli Defense Force (IDF) military bases. It is a one to three-week program, where you live on an army base with other volunteers. My job was in a medical supply warehouse.

We lived in the barracks, wore uniforms, and had our meals with active-duty soldiers, who were never without their assault weapons in the mess hall. That experience was as close to being in the army as I would ever get.

The living conditions were woefully lacking in comfort. I was the last of the five women to arrive at the barracks. The bunk beds had all been taken. They had claimed the bottom ones for sleeping and commandeered the top ones for their personal items. They also had requisitioned the upper mattresses or what passed as mattresses as they were no more than a two-inch synthetic foam laid over plywood. My plywood single cot was placed between two bunks that were against either wall. The crude bathroom facilities were outside, which made for quick steppin' when nature called in the dark of night.

Like *the Princess and the Pea*, if there was a pea, I would have felt it. I had not lived under such pathetic conditions since attending Camp Aya-po in the 1950s. That was a YWCA camp, which was run like a detention center for twelve-year-old girls, located somewhere in the dense valleys of Connecticut. I felt *Annie's* pain before she was saved by Daddy Warbucks.

My job at the IDF base was working in a warehouse, replacing and updating medical supplies in field bags for the medics. It was a responsibility that was taken and accomplished with the utmost diligence. I went to make a difference. By giving of myself, I had the exhilaration of a new and important way of contributing. I was impressed by the other volunteers, men and women from all over the world, Jew and Gentile from ages twenty-one to eighty.

Some of the work was physically challenging; lugging heavy bags, sorting them, and then stacking and packing them in large crates to be sent to medical fields and other bases, wherever necessary. Regardless of the rigorous work, I had no aches or pains at the end of the day, and speaking of the end of the day, that's when it became enjoyable. We came together, sharing the same values and living in the same bare-boned conditions, relaxing, and enjoying one another's company.

That was not anything I expected. I never gave a second thought to meeting men and women and initiating long-term relationships when I signed on, so it was a delightful bonus to get when you are giving of yourself. And now, years later, I still enjoy the friendships that were formed at the base.

 Wear your mini-sox inside out. They're softer and smoother than the inside stitching that feels like keloid scars on your feet. Who's going to see them when they are worn in your dark sweaty sneakers?

FORTY-ONE

Travel lots o'cities

When I first started to travel, like many of my contemporaries, I went to Europe and the UK. Been there, done that. Cobble-stone streets and picturesque cottage-style homes and the quaintness of old Europe no longer tempt me. Neither do the multitude of churches that speckle Europe like sand on a beach. I've been to enough European museums and gift shops to last whatever time I have left.

What does entice me, in my more recent travels, are the people. While visiting a Hindu temple in Southern India, my longtime travel pals, Gail and Stanley and I were the only pale faces in a sea of tens of thousands of dark-skinned people. We were stared at, and school-aged children, as we smiled at them in friendship, timidly came over to touch us. It made me mindful of what it feels like when you don't look like everyone else.

I like meeting people who don't believe or even know the same things. What's a Jew? Many of my newest acquaintances admitted they had never (or didn't know they had), met one. Really!!!

They dress differently. There was not a bare-footed person at the temple grounds that did not do a double-take on seeing my legs extending from my knee-length denim skirt to my socks' clad feet. The Indian women were covered from head to toe, their bare skin as rare as snow in Miami.

We speak different languages but at the same time, we can touch one another literally and figuratively. They love taking pictures. We all laughed at the same thing when looking at our selfie's. We hugged, feeling a genuine kinship.

We eat when we're hungry, albeit not the same food. We sleep when we're tired, but not with the same accommodations. We dress to cover ourselves, but not in similar styles. We shop for our necessities but not in the same way, as even our necessities vary. There are so many differences but, when you put us in a circle, we all come together. Many people I met have never seen an ocean. But then again, I've never seen the Matterhorn or the Altai Mountains of Siberia.

We, in the modern world, take so much for granted. Take away the superficial facades, the endless aisles of prepared foodstuff in the supermarkets, Amazon, and instant gratification, and we may learn that people in faraway places have more meaning in their lives. They may be the ones that stop and smell the roses; the ones who are connected to the earth, and the families they have time for.

They don't have the same outside influences that impact our lives; the things we take for granted. They don't throw things away…they don't waste. When I left a little food on my plate in a restaurant the waiter hesitated to remove it from the table. He looked askance that I would leave food, no matter how little. When you live in a country of 1.4 billion people, you don't waste food. Obviously, I never did that again

I started ticking off Africa, Asia, and Australia. The "3-A's" did offer a wider assortment of the unexpected until twelve-twenty plus hours of air travel became too tiring. *When did THIS happen?* It happened when I finally realized that "getting there" is not half the fun anymore. Flying, and dealing with the airlines has become tedious and uncomfortable.

Getting an AARP subscription was no longer what your mother received and then, lo and behold, as anyone can deal with a few hours on a plane, the travel suggestions for the U.S. and Canada suddenly had jet appeal.

Last but not least, not wanting to give up our creature comforts, we seniors discovered that cruising was, as Goldilocks said with a sigh of relief, "Just right." And besides, the seats on ships are much superior to plane seats.

Do we still have the stamina to make the travel arrangements, arrange for the cat or dog sitter, get someone to retrieve the mail, and change medical appointments? Can we be certain that our passport won't expire less than six months from the date we return, fill our save-a-life prescriptions, and contend with the myriad of other incidentals that need to be tended to while tripping the light fantastic in another country?

If it's hot, we need air-conditioning, if it's cold, well, we, at least in South Florida are certainly not gonna tolerate that!

We reach an age where countless travel programs on countless channels, watched on our super-sized flat TV screens in our comfy homes, satisfy us without piquing the desire to leave the womb of our La-Z-Boy recliners. Our minds travel anywhere via our TVs or laptops.

FORTY-TWO

Quirky Traveler

Q uirky tourists travel and explore, immersing themselves in local cultures, especially in, *off-the-beaten-track* destinations. They are amenable to trying new things, sampling local cuisine, accepting diverse lifestyles, and meeting new people. Sleeping, eating, and living with them rather than simply observing from a moving vehicle is what I call, "hands-on." Non-quirky tourists are easy to spot. They are the one's seeking information on how to say "Denny's" in a multitude of languages.

The typical tourist likes to sightsee. Their traveling is akin to being a spectator on wheels, being guided to museums, churches, and shops. They never venture down the side streets, or too far from "downtown."

Call me quirky. I find it more fun to be a participant even when it's something as simple as taking a cooking lesson in Jordan, learning how to prepare Mujadara, a mixture of rice, lentils, and spices. I could also go the more intense route by digging on an archaeological site, something I've yet to do unless you count the time excavating oyster shells and arrowheads in upstate New York.

Volunteering and working with pandas more than fulfilled my lifelong dream. I always assumed, at best, one day I might be watching them from an observation area in their natural environment or at a zoo, but nothing beats the reality of co-mingling and interacting with another species.

At the beginning of the 21st century, I recognized that the computer, like an older child accepting the new baby, was not going away. I attempted to conquer my trepidation to becoming "puter" literate, by searching for something that always fascinated me. I typed in *Pandas*.

Lo and behold, after many hits and misses, I found an organization offering volunteers the opportunity to go to a research center in Chengdu, China. That was a good *perk* for overcoming my fear of the unknown... learning the computer. And so, I went to the province of Sichuan, a land-locked area in southwest China, at the easternmost part of the Tibetan

Plateau. Now, years later, I no longer fear it, but I never did learn it. To this day, the 'puter' remains as confounding as finding Big Foot.

Babysitting fifteen orphaned baby monkeys proved to be the most demanding of all my volunteering jobs. They need the same twenty-four-hour attention as newborn humans, except monkeys don't wear diapers during the day. They spent their days climbing and pooping all over me and the other volunteers as we all shared the same enclosures in temps hovering around 100 degrees, or more, in South Africa.

I didn't expect that volunteering with the Sar-El program in Israel, working on a medical supply army base restocking medics bags would also include teaching my Hebrew speaking boss to speak English. He preferred learning slang and swear words, rather than conversational phrases, like I taught in Spain. While in Spain I worked with other volunteers from several English-speaking countries, conversing with young Spanish professionals who were striving to improve their English...doing what I do best, talking...in English, only.

For me, being *hands-on* is more interesting than being hauled around with a bus full of strangers, being driven from photo-op to photo-op. Not that there's anything wrong with that! It's far more exciting to be somewhere other than sitting home watching travel programs, although that's better than lounging on your couch watching your stocks go up and down, listening to the talking heads battle for viewer ratings.

Regardless, do something. Be part of the action, rather than sitting on the sidelines spending your life as an observer instead of a doer. You will have no regrets for pushing the envelope and being there. No more should've, could've, would've...when you make memories rather than regrets.

FORTY-THREE

Anagha and Me

Thrilled to be taking this momentous journey, leaving Miami International forty-five minutes late did not dampen my excitement. No big deal. Flying almost 9,000 miles, the pilot shouldn't have a problem making up the time. I gave no more thought to that, nor to the fifty-five minutes my Amex travel agent assured me was plenty of time to change planes in London's Heathrow Airport, since the next leg of the journey to Mumbai was on the same airline, Virgin Atlantic, and leaving from the same terminal. Seriously, what could go wrong?

Thanks to the frequent flyer miles I accrued by charging all my business expenses, I looked forward to savoring the next twenty hours in comfort. I changed out of my winter black travel clothes for the one size fits all, comfy, loose, sleep-set the airline offers business and first-class passengers for their overnight flights.

The flight was uneventful albeit, uncomfortable. The pod-like seating had two positions, straight up for sitting, or flat for sleeping. To look out the window you had to twist your body, as the seats faced into the cabin. If the person on the other side of the plane was also sitting up, you stared at each other. Hope the airline didn't overpay the designer.

Nine hours later, approximately fifty minutes before landing, the flight attendant announced, "All passengers going to Mumbai will be missing their connection due to our late arrival." I don't know why she felt compelled to use her mic as the only four people affected were, coincidently, sitting in business class and she was looking directly at us while making her announcement. We knew we were the only ones going to Mumbai as she told us so during our flight.

Years ago, connecting flights were held when the incoming plane was behind schedule; especially one on the same airline and leaving from the same terminal. This aircraft to Mumbai would only have needed to wait for a few minutes. Much later we discovered that that flight to Mumbai left a few minutes earlier than scheduled.

Upon our questioning, the flight attendant informed us we would be met at the gate and escorted to where we would wait for the next flight to Mumbai. She had no clue as to where and assured us, upon our desperate questioning, "Your luggage will be removed from this aircraft and delivered to the one you will be taking for the final leg of your journey. Due to security reasons, no luggage can be transported without its rightful owner." Yup!

The woman seated in the first row, directly in front of mine, stood up, protesting. She was told, emphatically we would be escorted to where we needed to go, and would definitely be on the next plane, which she assured us, would be leaving in the next hour or so, and "Absolutely, your luggage, is safe. Not to worry, no luggage flies alone." Right! I did the research and found out that 390,000 pieces of luggage "flew alone", or without their rightful owners, last year due to airline error.

We landed ten minutes late, which gave us forty-five minutes to de-plane, re-plane, and have our luggage put on the new flight. At the terminal, we parked next to our connecting flight which was sitting at the gate.

Fuhgeddaboudit. Upon deplaning we were met by a Virgin Atlantic representative. When we insisted that our connecting plane, which we pointed to through the glass window, was so close we could practically reach out and touch it had not yet left the terminal, our pleas fell on deaf ears. I was later told by my Amex travel rep "Off the record, they were not going to hold a flight, no matter how few minutes, for one American and three Indian women"

The young woman I had flown with, and I, introduced ourselves to each other. We walked together, behind the VA rep while the other two women, a woman, and her niece, trailed behind, prattling in a language I did not recognize. I assumed all Indians spoke English, albeit with a heavy accent. *Guess again stupida, they do not.*

I was sticking by my new friend, Anagha, a young attractive Indian woman in her mid-thirties, who spoke Hindi and English. We walked, and we walked, and then we walked some more. We must have made quite a picture; this tired rag-tag foursome in our sleep-sets, lugging large hand-bags with only the squeaks of our rubber-soled shoes echoing through the cold empty terminals.

Thirty minutes later we arrived at a bus stop. Still at the airport, but now outside, in the damp, dark, London late-autumn air. The rep directed us as to what to do. "When the bus comes," and at what terminal we were to "de-bus," and "go to the Air India counter." Doing an about-face, with nary a pleasant English 'Cheerio', she gave us a curt, "Goodbye", and disappeared as if a wisp of smoke.

We de-bused at the large, cold, dimly lit, and at 4 a.m., deserted, terminal. The two Indian women stayed on our heels, chattering, and not introducing themselves. Once again, we traversed the airport.

Passing rows of empty airline counters, there was no sign for Air India. Near the end of the terminal, Anagha spotted a narrow hallway off to the right, and at the end, was a small hand-printed sign over a makeshift counter, *Air India*.

She spoke to the clerk in Hindi, as he spoke no English. He was unaware of our saga. Finally, he sorted it out and confirmed us on a direct Air India flight leaving in two hours.

Anagha explained to him I needed to connect with a flight on another airline to Jaipur upon landing. Silently he stared at me.

Try as she did, she could not convince him to assist me even after showing him my pre-paid, confirmed ticket. The aunt and niece curled up under their winter coats to ward off the unheated, damp, dimly lit waiting area. All the shops were shuttered closed so we couldn't even buy a bottle of water.

Anagha called her husband, Vivek, who was home in Mumbai and asked him to check on flights to Jaipur. He called back exclaiming, "No one is answering." It was the middle of the night there.

During our wait, she called the guest home in Jaipur. She informed the Hindi-speaking owner that I might not be on my scheduled flight and please notify my travel pals Gail and Stanley, who were flying in from Jacksonville, and hopefully did not meet my same fate. Tell them I was okay and would get myself to the guest house if I did not meet them, as we had pre-arranged, at the Mumbai airport.

Although I was arriving about three hours later than scheduled, there was still a possibility we could rendezvous at the domestic terminal and continue on to Jaipur together. These phone calls were not without the frustrations of dropped calls and bad connections. There were also charges for the time used, and not everyone, at that time, was wirelessly connected.

Arriving in Mumbai eleven hours later...IF I could retrieve my luggage, which had been red- ticketed "Priority" when I had checked in in Miami, and IF I quickly found a cab to take me to the domestic terminal which was thirty minutes away, I still might be able to catch my flight to Jaipur. Yup, like that was gonna happen!

The luggage carousel came to a screeching halt after all the luggage was removed, leaving four exhausted ladies, still in their sleep sets standing there, empty-handed except for auntie and niece clutching their winter coats.

Hours after landing, the clerk in charge of lost luggage finally completed filling in the forms during our Q&A. We all had to answer individually, while reams of paper fed from the box on the floor under the printer spilled over the printer and piled up back on the floor. After he typed, typed, typed, very slow, slow, slow, with two fingers, one by one we were questioned, especially me, about why we were traveling. "I am going to work with elephants," I told Anagha. God knows how she translated and explained that.

Finally, I was given my testimony to sign. I didn't have a clue as to what he typed, the print being too light to read. There wasn't ink in the printer and besides, I assumed it was in Hindi since he spoke no English. How could there be no ink in a country that has an ink named after it? By this time, I had missed my flight to Jaipur.

Now we had to "wait for other officials to come." We were not allowed to leave. There was not a chance of, let's say, going outside for a cigarette and forgetting to come back since we were being surveilled by four military men armed with assault weapons.

Auntie and the niece, who never interacted with us during this entire debacle, finally were allowed to leave. Mumbai was their destination, as was Anagha's. It was now past 3 a.m. She mentioned she had to be at work in a few hours.

I said goodbye and thanked her for being so helpful. She looked me straight in the eye and in no uncertain terms said, "I am not leaving you." She directed me to the escalator, and we rode up to the main terminal only to find it was deserted. "Stay here!" she ordered. Like Alice scurrying down the rabbit hole, I watched as she was swallowed up on the down escalator.

What's a nice lady like me, at the age of seventy-something, doing here? In a sleep-set? With no luggage? At 4 a.m. in the departure terminal of the Chhatrapati Shivaji International Airport, in Mumbai, India, a country where over one billion, three hundred fifty thousand people call home, I am the only one here. Where is everybody?

Nervously waiting for, what seemed like forever, but could not have been more than twenty minutes, I jumped for joy when Anagha reappeared, dragging a disheveled young man with her, who looked like had been asleep. She instructed him to sell me a ticket on the next plane to Jaipur. Finally, we walked out in the cool night air. Again, I thanked her profusely and asked where to get the bus that left for the domestic airport every half hour. She looked at me, again saying firmly, "I am not leaving you."

Her husband, who had been waiting outside, insisted on driving me. Thirty minutes later, Vivek parked the car outside the domestic terminal, escorted me to the Spicejet Airline counter. Spicejet is purportedly India's "favorite domestic airline." He waited while I checked in and remained to ensure there were no hitches or glitches. Anagha called the owner of the guest home again when she knew what flight I was on and arranged for him to pick me up at the Jaipur airport.

She and I stayed in touch during my time in Jaipur and made a date to meet when I returned to Mumbai. I wrote to Anagha's employer about my overwhelming appreciation. My gratitude to her and her husband transcended and spilled over to other Indians I met. I visited them on subsequent visits to India and she has come to Florida. Thanks to social media, and *WhatsApp* we stay connected. She and her family are my friends for life.

As a postscript, I had to take a tuk-tuk to the airport to retrieve my luggage which arrived five days later. So, you see, luggage does travel alone. My bag had been opened and then shrink-wrapped. It had stickers and tags on it from at least five different airports and countries I never heard of.

It reached me with the final tag, marked "crew." So much for no luggage left behind. Next year, I plan to travel to all the places my suitcase has been…

FORTY-FOUR

Jaipur

I came to Jaipur volunteering to work with elephants. Landing at the beautiful modern Jaipur airport, I was met by Dinshaw, the owner and our host of the Prity House, named after one of his daughters.

Their guest house would be my home for the next week. After offering him a tip for the extra trip he had to make, he politely but firmly refused it.

Women, in brightly colored sarees, stooped over short-handled home-made brushes, were sweeping the pavement of the immaculate and beautifully groomed thoroughfare leading from the airport. Wow! What a pleasant surprise from the gloom and doom I was expecting after well-intentioned friends exploited INDIA as an acronym for, *I'll Never Do India Again.*

Without warning, the manicured land and the bright flowered landscape ended abruptly. The center divider was gone, and the sides of the road no longer were ablaze with magnificent splashes of nature's best. In a blink of an eye the scenic road ended and, as if I was carried off on a flying carpet, I landed back in the first century.

Dinshaw's car kicked up clouds of choking dust as he navigated around potholes and free-roaming animals who shared the road, as if just another vehicle. He beeped through the din of honking horns, bleating calves, squealing pigs and throngs of beautifully garbed women balancing large bags on their heads, their colorful sarees electrifyingly the dusty landscape. They were shopping for pungent herbs, spices, and vegetables, or were the vendors, squatting at the edge of the road behind their piled high vegetables.

This was the India I had anticipated from seeing countless documentaries. What couldn't be felt in my pre-judged images in darkened rooms thousands of miles away, was the awakening of my senses in the center of this universe of authentic sounds, smells, and textures.

After plowing through a living diorama of humanity and mammals, we eventually turned left onto a quiet residential side street, and then made a quick right. In the middle of the block, in front of a two-story simple dwelling on the left side of the street, the signpost read, The Prity House.

Dinshaw led me into an open foyer where cases of bottled water were stacked high on the left. Beyond that, a motorcycle, which I learned later belonged to Prity, one of the hosts' daughters, a very pretty woman barely out of her teens. To the right was a small sink, and a well-worn sofa where Gail and Stanley sat looking like cats that ate the canaries, anxiously waiting to see how I would react to the ride…and now the house.

On the first floor was a large reception area, a dining area, and off to the left, a curtained small utilitarian kitchen. At the back of the house was a large bedroom where most of the family slept. Upstairs had a row of four bedrooms. I was shown to the front one, facing the street

It had walls, a bed, and a bathroom- with a bucket, experience. I was happy to have arrived- Oh yeah, except for that whole suitcase thing.

From that moment on, my travel buds, Gail, Stanley, and I lived authentically and traditionally Indian, from the removal of our shoes at the door to personal hygiene. This truly was a paperless society. We came prepared with handi-wipes, soap, Kleenex, and toilet paper. Buckets for water served for washing and toilet flushing. Cie la vie!

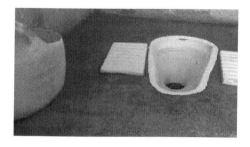

Living harmoniously, yet seemingly centuries apart, many Indians maintain their culture by living traditional lives, while others embrace the modern world. Our hosts were definitely not part of the latter.

On our first evening, we attended an outdoor dining establishment complete with sitar music. Exotic and wonderful dialects from families sharing their own ground level feasts drifted around and above us. The aroma of countless spices that create the uniqueness of Indian food, was a hospitable introduction to what was an amazing visit.

Sitting barefoot and cross-legged and served by a barefoot waiter who stood attentively above us, it was my first-time eating dinner on a colorful tapestry cloth covering sandy ground.

In this village-like setting were vendors within lighted stalls. Although the paths were lit, what attracted me was the flawless night sky. I felt like I was under an astronomically deep indigo canopy filled with infinite crystal-like flickering stars. It was awe inspiring.

I awoke every day at 4:30 a.m., excited to start the day. Fifteen minutes later our transportation, a three-wheel yellow and green tuk-tuk chugged up to the Prity House.

In the cold, darkness, we were driven to the outskirts of Jaipur. Our driver, as well as the few others, traversing past the barely visible outlines of buildings on the unlit streets, blasted their horns at anything and everything. It didn't seem to matter that most Jaipurians were still asleep. One small headlight on the front of the tuk-tuks barely penetrated the blue-black ambience.

We rocked and rolled through mostly deserted streets. One morning we barely made out the dark silhouettes of women on the side of the road chanting and parading. Another day we saw the figures of men, who we assumed were going to work.

Stanley, Gail, and I sat on the hard narrow bench behind the driver. Trying to get warm, we huddled, our behinds cheek to cheek to cheek.

Every day, we were taken on a different route. We weaved in and out of streets, lanes, alleys, and an occasional driveway. The air became colder and damp as we rode along the many lakes and rivers that butted up against the roadways.

Occasionally, we smelled strange smelling burnings as we traveled. We hoped it was only garbage. Our driver couldn't tell us. He didn't speak English.

FORTY-FIVE

The Golden Girls

N ever will I forget that first morning. Our driver announced our arrival with incessant horn blowing. While waiting for the massive wooden medieval looking doors to swing open, the wailing of the muezzin (A man who calls Muslims to prayer from the minaret of a mosque) summoning the worshippers through the city-wide loudspeakers cast its spiritual spell.

We stood, transfixed, surrounded by darkness, shivering in the dry desert-like air as splinters of light began yawning brighter as the doors opened slowly from within, illuminating an enormous concrete barn, known as the '*Elephant Palace*'.

Inside were four turban- clad young men in sarong style clothing, or long shirts called Kurtas. The ones not barefoot wore sandals. Gail, Stanley, and I deferentially stepped in. The men, called mahouts, who tend and live with the elephants, seemed riveted in place as they stared at us, our mouths agape, mesmerized by this near-psychedelic diorama.

There were six full grown female elephants. Three of them faced into the center, while the three on the left looked out towards the window openings. We were awed by the spectacle of this spiritual, peaceful, living tableau.

The mahouts explained, in very broken English, that our chores would entail caring for the three cows (female elephants) who were facing us. The other three facing out were new to the barn and hadn't acclimated yet to be 'trusted' around us ... nor us around them.

Some days, when we arrived, the 'girls' were asleep, lying on their sides, curled up in fetal positions. They became our Rose, Dorothy and Blanche, *The Golden Girls*. Being hands on with these magnificent creatures allowed us to see how golden they truly were.

Over the next five days, we got to hear Rose snore, watch Dorothy drool as she slept, and see Blanche, sound asleep, with a stick of sugar cane curled up in her trunk like a pacifier. On the second day, the girls' stretched out their trunks in greeting and... were they actually smiling!? I was in love.

Besides cleaning and refreshing their stalls, we made them chapatti, an Indian flat bread. One afternoon while giving them their snacks, the mahout instructed me to feed Blanche by putting a small bundle of freshly cut wheat tied with a piece of plant resembling clover, directly into her mouth. I watched as Dorothy was fed a bundle in her trunk which she rolled neatly into her mouth.

Blanche kept extending her trunk to me, wanting to receive her snack the way the others did. I didn't see what harm there would be, so I let her scoop up the bundle in my hand with her trunk. Wildly she swung it over her head and started swatting herself on the back, making a mess. The mahout came running over, yelling at her to stop playing with her food.

She gave me a contemptuous, 'It's your fault' look. I whispered into her flapping ear, "Don't blame me for trying."

We worked from 5:30 a.m. 'til 11:30. As we cleaned their stalls, we talked to them. They were aware that we really cared for them. We fed them and assisted in getting the riders' baskets on their backs for their day's work, carrying visitors up the side of the mountain to the Amber Palace. Built in 1592, it is a fort famous for its artistic Hindu design and a 'must-see' attraction for Indians and foreigners alike.

Tuk-tuking back to the Prity House, passing our girls led by the mahouts on their way to work, we called out, "Have a good day." Turning, they acknowledged us by nodding their massive heads.

On our last day, after finishing our chores, we were treated to a ride on our part time wards. Riding high past residential homes, thinking the neighboring homes had concrete walls for protection, to my surprise some of the neighbors had their own elephants!

From the mystical experience of being up close and personal with the largest land mammals on earth and seeing firsthand their intelligence and gentleness, one can only hope that they will be allowed to survive in the wild forever.

While with the girls, I forgot the outside world, but was jolted back to reality upon returning to the guest house and, frustratingly, calling Amex every day. On the fifth day I was told my luggage was "located". We were so deep in the 'hood, the locator, not knowing how to reach me, refused to deliver it. I hired a tuk-tuk and spent hours going and coming back from the airport.

My return from the airport was like Christmas in October. For five days I wore my airline sleep set and one change of undies that I had in my carry- on bag. I washed those out and hung them on the window handle to dry every night. The only clothing available in the part of town where we were living were sarees and I was not about to wear a sari and my sneakers to sweep dung from under the elephants.

Gail and Stanley sat cross-legged at the foot of my bed as I slashed away at the shrink-wrapped goodies with a scissors and knife. My companions eagerly awaited the treats I promised I had packed; the most important item being my roll of toilet paper, since I had 'borrowed 'a roll of theirs. We devoured my Lances' Peanut Planks. They ogled my soap, but it was too small to cut and share. I joyfully reconnected with my travel weary denim burial skirt, which has flown more miles than I, for more than thirty years, and I have requested to wear it on my final journey from this life to the next. With my tee shirts, and a baseball cap to protect against the unrelenting sunny days, I was thrilled to cast away the sleep set!

During our free afternoons we strolled through the bazaars in the center of town. Although we bundled up for the cold, damp, and about 40 degrees Fahrenheit mornings, by the time we returned 'home' the temperature soared to a dry, 100 degrees plus under an unrelenting sun in a cloudless blue sky.

The city was alive with movement, color, sounds and fragrances. The women's brilliantly colored sarees sparkled against the backdrop of the men in white shirts and black pants. The crowds and the rich aroma of vendors' fresh and pungent spices made my mouth water, and the cacophony of the incessant bleating horns and rushing traffic reminded me, "You're no longer in Kansas, Dorothy."

Walking with the masses on footpaths we crisscrossed with monkeys, pigs, camels, oxen, and the sacred cows, who always had the right-of-way. We avoided the feral dogs who showed no interest in us or other dogs. Like a well-choreographed ballet, no matter how busy or crowded the streets, no human or animal brushed or bumped into one another.

A snake charmer sat cross-legged, who, I thought, existed only in folklore. We watched as the charmer gave the cobra a "tap" on his head with his lute to start him uncoiling from his basket.

My writing allows me to step through the looking glass and relive my experiences as though they are taking place this very moment. Photographs, although beautiful, may fade in time. The sights, smells, the atmosphere…oh, if only to be able to time travel; to go back to those days and nights. I would not change a single thing.

FORTY-SIX

The Groom's Party

For two consecutive evenings we went with Mike, a fellow guest, to a local hotel for Happy Hour. He was volunteer teaching twenty boys in an orphanage. On the second night, we were greeted like long lost friends by the hotel host who insisted we ascend to the roof to observe a show of Indian women dancing. We relaxed and danced with the dancers and each other.

Our host at the Prity House invited us to "my brother's son's" Groom's Party. To get us ready, one of our host's daughters, Pooja, painted beautiful henna designs on my hands, arms, and legs.

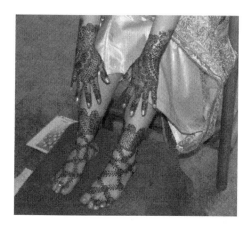

We ten guests were driven to the other side of Jaipur. What a scene it was as we entered the home. Five women, all brilliantly dressed in sarees, were sitting on the floor on a large cloth upon which were aromatic boiling pots of breads and other food items. We were served at a picnic style table outdoors in the side yard. We said, in jest, all that was missing was some liquor. The uncle sidled up to the table and offered us some spirits. We all graciously, refused it. Although a drink or two seemed very appropriate at this event, we weren't certain we wouldn't be offending any of our hosts if alcohol was not legal in this part of the country. None of the other people were imbibing.

The festivities took on a life of its own, growing, and glowing. At least one hundred men, women, children, and babies in their mothers' arms entered the yard.

As evening turned to night we watched as the groom-to-be showed up on a white steed outside the fenced-in yard. We followed the crowd. The groom's young nephew sat in front of him on the saddle of his ornately decorated white stallion.

Following behind, was a band made up of horns and drums. Everyone paraded around the neighborhood on unlit, dusty, unpaved roads. I was literally held up by two young men; one of whom lit the way with his cell-phone flashlight through the ebony darkness.

Lots of the men, women, and especially the children were excited by the sight of my digital camera. They wanted their picture taken, which I did happily and then showed them the photos. Some of them posed with me.

As we circled the streets, a few of the residents invited the revelers into their beautiful homes. It was an incredible evening that began at 6 p.m. and was still going strong when we reluctantly left six hours later.

Pooja offered to take me home on her motorcycle. As tempting as that was, I declined after a possible news headline flashed in my head. *Elderly woman killed in India while riding on a motorcycle, at midnight. What was she thinking?* Living among the local people and sharing in this pre- wedding celebration gave us a taste of Indian culture that was...priceless.

Because of our schedule, we had to miss the wedding. It was an arranged marriage of a young woman whom we did not meet. The next day Gail, Stanley, and I were picked up in a *real* car at 6 a.m. for our ride to Agra.

FORTY-SEVEN

Agra and Varanasi

More than the trinkets were the priceless, unforgettable memories I brought home that further heightened my fascination with the people I met in this mystical country.

Soon after leaving the chaos of Jaipur City at 6 a.m., we entered a modern-day highway with almost no traffic for the four-hour ride to Agra, home of the Taj Mahal. The rising sun quickly heated the barren fields and the air settled over us like a brown woolly cloak. Adding to the pollution were men making and baking bricks on the sides of the road. A timeless scene, the brick-making method and routine the same as it was a thousand years ago.

We arrived at the Trident Hotel in Agra. Coming from the Prity House to the 21st century had its advantages. Cold and HOT running water, as well as everything we expect modern-day lodgings to have, except we could have been anywhere in the world. No matter how luxurious, a hotel is a hotel, although the attentiveness of the employees and the indigenous food was in keeping with the Indian hospitality we enjoyed.

That afternoon we visited Agra Fort, built about a hundred years earlier than the Taj. It is the size of a small city and is completely contained within red sandstone walls. I stood on the balcony where, we were told, Shah Jahan watched over his memorial. Marveling at the magnificent structure five miles away, the Taj Mahal looked like an enchanted shrine plucked out of a mystical fairy tale.

In 1632, Shah Jahan had commissioned a mausoleum to be built for Mumtaz Mahal. She was the favorite of his three wives and died at the age of thirty-eight giving birth to their fourteenth child. Exiled to the Fort by one of his four sons, the Shah spent the last eight years of his life there. Looking at the two living quarters of the Shah, I must admit, Mel Brooks is still right, "It's good to be king."

Our young guide extolled contagious enthusiasm and seemed to be informed, although his heavy Indian accent often made his narrative difficult to comprehend. The Shah had more than three hundred concubines who lived on the first level, while his three wives had their separate chambers on the second level. If you do the math, you will see that the Shah had enough female companions to spend time with a different one each night of the year...with Sundays off. Yes, it is good to be king, or in this place, Shah.

Jahan was dethroned by his sons, for his openness and freedom for all people regardless of their beliefs and faith...including his concubines, of course. The guide went on to explain that one wife was Catholic, from Portugal. I noticed, near the ceiling in her chamber, chiseled into the stone wall over the window opening, were three large Jewish stars. When I pointed them out, asking what the significance was, he paused, looked at them as though he was seeing them for the first time, and murmured, "They are decorations." You think?!

The Taj Mahal took 22,000 workers more than twenty years to build what has become the world's most famous romantic mausoleum and one of the most photographed sites on the globe. I watched the curtain of nightfall tenderly encompass the flawless, glowing white marble. No man-made illumination is needed to see its flawless resplendence, surrounded by the quietness of the night.

The following day we flew to Varanasi, a 3,000-year-old, continuously occupied city on the banks of the Ganges River. On the ride from the airport to our hosts home, I had to cover my face to shield myself from the air teeming with brown dust as we drove past countless impoverished families living in tarp-covered lean-to's lining the road. The scene was especially jarring after the splendor of the pristine Taj Mahal.

No matter how poor the areas were, there was the anomaly of the children in stylish, Ralph Lauren-styled school uniforms going to (religious) school, either packed into tuk-tuks or squeezed into small school busses.

Mr. and Mrs. Kapur warmly welcomed us with ceremonial marigold leis and served a traditional vegetarian Indian dinner. At sunrise, Mr. Kapur drove us to the Ganges for a boat ride on the river. Women, looking like sprinkled confetti dressed in their colorful sarees, were spreading washed white sheets to dry on the banks of the river.

Bathers, from the very young to the elderly, splashed and enjoyed the river. The smoke drifting from the seemingly serene images emanating from the cremations above the river formed a circle of life. Since my visit, new protective laws forbidding the discarding of city and industrial waste into the river and no longer allowed the dumping of idols, or ashes from dead bodies, the river is now at its cleanest point in many decades.

With Mr. Kapur leading the way, we weaved through the city above the Ganges. The buildings had all been constructed high above the water line to avoid flooding during the Monsoons. The streets, more like narrow alleyways, were constructed to twist and turn, thus protecting the citizens from invaders.

In the evening we returned to experience the spiritual fire ritual ceremony of Ganga Aarti which is performed daily to honor the River Goddess Ganga.

Mrs. Kapur was an excellent cook and was delighted that we devoured everything she put in front of us.

Some of her (simpler) recipes are:

Tomato Soup*

7-8 tomatoes

Cup water

Cabbage, one or two carrots

Boil all, puree, and boil again.

Add a pinch of salt and pepper and a little sugar.

Add cream to serve

*This one I would go by taste and what feels right.

Potato Pancakes

Six potatoes boiled and mashed

½ Cup tapioca which needs to be soaked one or
    two hours

Fresh coriander or mint leaves.

Fry in sunflower or olive oil.

(a slight variation on traditional latkes)

Carrot Salad

Grate carrots

Add little salt and lemon juice. Add fresh
    pomegranates or ones in a jar if not available.

Chapatti, no recipe.

I think it's flour and water fried in vegetable oil.

    Yum.

*Mrs. Kapur's English was difficult to understand, so please do not write a letter to this author. Her recipes included 'a pinch of this, about a cup or two of that, one or two tsp, etc.

The next day we hired a driver to take us to a small quiet town to visit a Hindu Temple. As we were exiting our car, two clean-cut young boys, dressed in clean khaki pants and crisp white shirts, who appeared to be about ten years old, rushed over to the car, waving trinkets and beads. My friends walked ahead. I walked slower, taking in the things the boys were waving in front of my face.

"No, not now. When we come out, we will look and see if there's anything we want to buy." I didn't want to disappoint them by saying we would and then not do so. One of the boys said something I didn't understand. He was trying to get my attention to show me what he was holding. I said, brushing him aside, "No, thank you." He persisted. I stopped, suddenly recognizing what he had in his hand.

I looked over and said, "Is this your wallet, Stanley?" He stopped walking and felt his pocket where he kept it. It was empty. He walked back to where I was standing with the boys and took it from his outstretched hand.

A mile before, we had stopped to buy bottles of water. Stanley bought them, and apparently, he missed putting the wallet back in his pocket, which fell in the gutter of the road when he got out of the car at the temple. He offered the boy some rupees. The young boy smiled, shook his head, and held up his trinkets. The three of us told him, "Before we leave, we promise we will buy something."

When we left the temple, they were waiting. The second boy offered me a necklace. I told him I was going to buy it from his friend, the one who found the wallet and turned to buy it from him. The first boy, hearing what I said, turned and implored me, "Please, buy it from him, he asked you first." The boys made their sales, but what they might never know was the goodwill they made.

Long after the gifts I bought will have been forgotten, what I will never forget was their honesty and loyalty to one another. It certainly was a most unexpected and pleasant experience.

I think I am going to skip my next trip because I'm so exhausted from your last one.

Cousin Michael

FORTY-EIGHT

Evening in Paris

ettled in my reclining seat on the final leg of my journey, I felt the vodka and tonic I had just savored start to take ownership of my mind and body. Hopefully, its effect would help me lapse, at least for some of the eight-hours, into neverland during my overnight flight to Delhi, on my third trip to India. As my eyes fluttered closed, my mind drifted back to the last twenty-four hours...

While I was checking into the Hotel de Crillon, I noticed him off to one side of the lobby, seated at his Louis XIV desk.

He was a slim attractive Indian gentleman with a bronze skin tone that glowed under the silver-gray hair that skirted his shirt collar. I noted his name on the brass nameplate, Robin LaPak, *Bonne Volonte'* (*willingness, readiness, helpfulness*). Giving me an affable smile as our eyes met while passing him on my way to the lift, he stopped me and engaged in conversation.

"Yes. I just arrived from Miami. I'm on my way to Delhi, I will be leaving tomorrow at midnight. Since Air France stops in Paris, what better place to indulge me than the Crillon?"

"Are you traveling alone?"

I assured him I was and detected a hint of coyness when he asked, "May I come by and make sure everything is satisfactory for your overnight stay?" He told me he was a partner of this elegant Paris hotel. His function was to ensure that every guest be treated with the utmost care.

As I was standing on one of the two Juliet balconies, enjoying the view of the Champs Elysees and the Arc de Triomphe, I heard a soft knock at the door. "Oui," I responded.

I recognized the voice when he answered in English, "It is me." Opening the door, I took a step back. It was, indeed, Robin LaPak. He said softly, "You had me at '*Bon jour*." Gazing at me, I could feel his baby blue eyes melting my clothes away as he stepped in…quietly closing the door.

We took the few steps that separated us. I detected a beguiling hint of a men's cologne as he put his warm hands on my shoulders, drawing me, ever so gently, to him. It was as though I sensed his fingers, rather than felt them touching me. My body responded before my mind; the ecstasy swelling within me. It was like liquid gold warming every crevice of my body.

He slowly unbuttoned and peeled off my cream-colored silk blouse. As if in a trance, I watched as it floated slowly down to the cool, white, marble floor. I strained, needing to be touched, wanting to be kissed. He caressed my breasts, still sheathed in my lacy bra. I unbuttoned my black skirt, letting it fall to the floor. He took my hand in his and led me silently to the king-size bed.

He pulled back the fresh ivory comforter, but not before we embraced, our bodies melding and intertwining; our legs and arms becoming one. His kisses were warm on my face, my neck, my shoulders, and my breasts. I closed my eyes feeling the warm moisture of his tongue slowly reaching, barely touching, then lightly grazing the inside of my mouth as if he were trying to reach my inner soul…which he did.

We sank onto the bed with its cool, satiny sheets, my head nesting into the soft-down pillows. Stretched out beside me, he lightly played with my skin which responded as if it were electrically charged.

He continued to kiss every part of my body. His hands, sliding behind my back, effortlessly unhooking my bra, slipping the straps off my shoulders as slow as the hands of a schoolroom clock. I felt his warm breath and my nipples harden as he sucked them with his soft moist lips. He unhurriedly slid down the bed, not letting any part of my body go untouched, or void of gentle kisses. He slipped off my panties, letting them fall to the floor as he stared at me intently.

I was aware of his heart beating against my body, feeling his hardness as he entered me, we became one. His gyrations made me want him to plunge deeper, painfully deeper. Our passion slowly rose to a crescendo and he held me tight as we climaxed together. I felt his manliness flood inside me. He held me in his arms, neither one of us wanting this moment to slip away ... and it didn't.

As the late afternoon sun silently slipped into the western sky, darkness came upon us like a soft blanket. Hours later, we awakened and again enjoyed our intimacy, enhanced by the jasmine-scented breeze wafting through the open doors, floating above and through us.

At daybreak, Robin ordered strawberries and cream, freshly squeezed orange juice, croissants, and rich coffee steaming through frothy milk. On the breakfast tray was a spray of lilacs, my favorite flower.

After indulging ourselves, we drifted off into a deliciously deep sleep. I don't know how long I slept but when I awoke the sun was directly overhead, the room clean, and I was alone. The only reminiscence of last evening was the sweet fragrance of the lilacs in the exquisite silver bud vase sitting on the bedside table…that image fading as sleep once again took over my body.

FORTY-NINE

Ship Ahoy!

After exploring cobblestoned foreign countries by foot, I decided to walk on water by doing what so many of my contemporary's do, cruise. A few ladies from the 'hood invited me to join them for a seven-day all-you-can-eat Caribbean cruise. Easy peasy...or so I thought.

How will I keep myself lean?
With all the boat's tempting cuisine
Booze, buy, and binges
All things good and bad
come to an end
as well as all the cruises

Not wanting to miss a moment onshore, two of my traveling companions and I disembarked our floating mini-city, the 3,000 plus passenger *MSC Divine*, as soon as it docked, and the crew connected the gangway. It was 9 a.m. Welcome to St. John's on Antigua.

During the previous day at sea, most of the faithful cruisers were overly enthusiastic about hearing the ship's social director's sales pitch on shopping. The travelers reminded me of a puppy greeting you with yelps of excitement when you return from taking out the garbage.

The newbies as well as those well-seasoned cruisers overflowed the theatre. They came ready to be entertained and informed with a live program dedicated to the blessed day to come, aka shopping and an invitation to join the ship's VIP Shopping Party, "complimentary, of course."

We learned, and were shown a slide show, of all "the luxury items available, including Rolex, Cartier, Bulgari and many more at incredible "never-before-seen" prices! Having shopped 'til I dropped decades ago, and maybe even days ago, I opted to forgo this 'once in a cruise opportunity'.

We hired a local guide for a three-hour tour of the island. He left us, at our request, in the middle of downtown, in the heart of the boat people's shopping frenzy. Armed with the map that had been supplied free of charge by the local merchants to all the attendees at yesterdays' program, I left my friends to their shopping blitz and went in search of *Natura Creations*. This shop was sanctioned by the ship with its, *Only the stores on this map are backed by the shopping guarantee*. What the hell is a "shopping guarantee?"

The map showed the store is a block and a half away from the sanctioned area, but, in cruising and shopping terms on a strange island, that translated to light-years from the civilized safety zone. I assumed, by the name of the store they would have something more to offer beyond the unavoidable and insufferable. 'I ♥ Antigua souvenirs.

The first store I came to on the same street as *Natura Creations*, beckoned me. Taking a step in I could see mostly Rastafarian items including T-shirts and rasta caps, the round crocheted caps large enough for 'tucking in your dreadlocks,' plus your purse, your passport, and your lunch.

When asked, "What are you *wasn't* looking for?" I was certain it *wasn't* anything Rastafarian. Most of the time, when browsing, and asked what I am looking for, my fixed reply is, in a bright breezy voice that only me thinks is cute and catchy is, "Something that has my name on it." You know, something like this…

In other words, something that jumps out at me and begs; "Buy me, you won't be sorry. I promise I won't be a *wwit* when you get me home." What's a wwit? It's an acronym for, "What was I thinking?"What **WAS** I Thinking!

The second store was void of any customers, as was the first one. I spied a T-shirt with a bling message across the chest. After looking through all the sizes, colors, and styles, there was nothing with, "My name on it."

The lovely, friendly, young, salesgirl, Tamesha, offered, "I can take you to the place where they make the shirts. They'll be able to make a shirt in your size and print the message you want on it…and the prices are lower."

"Oh!" I exclaimed. She now had my full and undivided attention. Being on foreign soil on my own, although I was optimistic, it was with a smattering of pessimism.

"Where is this place?"

"Oh, just to the corner, across the street and on the left side of the next street. It's the yellow building. You can see it from here." I looked but didn't see what she was pointing to. That didn't stop me. She led the way up the street, crossing over the main street and then a side street. The building was on a corner with an outside stairway at the rear, on the street-side. Up the stairs we trudged. Intellectually, my left brain said, *Don't go. Quiet!* Right brain said, *It's okay, as long as it's not too deep in the building.*

At the second doorway, peering in, I saw that the walls were covered with shelves holding lots and lots of T-shirts. We walked in. Tamesha left with nary a *toodle-oo.* The two saleswomen, both in their mid-thirties, were pleasant, friendly, and helpful.

Like Goldilocks, after trying on shirts that were too big or too small, I found one that was jusssst right. Now, what color? *Can't go wrong with navy.* When it came to the design, I told her, "Bling," and pointed to a completed shirt. She told me she didn't have any more of that design. She continued doing her work, pressing designs on shirts. I spied something I liked.

I held up a tank top. "Do you have this design?"

The other woman said, "I will look." By now about half an hour had passed and I began thinking I was wearing out my welcome. *Hmmm, maybe I'll buy a few shirts to pay for my time spent here.*

Saved! Now I can leave. A couple came in with their teenage son looking at shirts for the gentleman. The sales lady obligingly began taking down men's shirts from the wall behind the counter with a long pole with a hook on the end. I waited for my lady to finish pressing designs on two T-shirts before she got to the one I selected. I had asked when I arrived "How much are the shirts?"

"Fifteen *dollas*." I thought *this is "wholesale?* They were fifteen *dollas* every-where. Oh well, mine will be customized.

She ironed on my selected blowfish with bubbles design. I asked the price again and if she would do better for cash rather than a credit card.

She looked directly into my eyes and stoically repeated, "Fifteen *dollas.*"

I handed her a ten-dollar bill and unfolded the dog-eared tuck on the upper right side of the five-dollar bill as it had become creased in my wallet. I watched her put the five-dollar bill and then the ten on top in the cash register drawer. She gave me my shirt in a small black plastic bag. I thanked her and acknowledged the other woman who was busy helping the man find a button-down loose-fitting shirt to fit over his bloated boat belly.

I walked down the stairs heading towards the main street having lost interest in finding *Natura Creations*. Suddenly, and without warning, there was a firm tap on my shoulder. Wheeling around I came face to face with Tamesha. I gave her a recognition smile. "You didn't pay me for the shirt", she accused.

"Huh?"

When she introduced me to her compatriots on the second-floor shirt shop I assumed she would be getting a kickback or commission but that was not my business. Surprised, I replied, "I paid the lady who waited on me."

She retorted, "No, you didn't. Come back with me." Wanting to resolve any misunderstanding and that I had, in fact, paid, I followed her back to the yellow two-storied building and up the stairs. She queried the women, "Did she pay for the shirt?"

"No!" both salesladies answered in unison.

I prevailed on the boat people who were about to wind up their transaction. "Didn't you see me pay the lady?"

"We weren't paying any attention and we don't want to get involved," said the man.

They turned to the saleslady and as they started to pay, uttered, "I hope we're not going to have a problem."

"No", she assured them as she took their cash. Before she put their money in, I had asked her to open the register. She ignored my request.

I repeated, "Open the register. You will see a ten-dollar bill and under it a five-dollar bill with an angled crease on the upper right corner."

"I've put money in since you were here, "she sneered.

"No, no one came here in the few minutes since I left. Open the register," I repeated. Nothing. I now demanded," OPEN THE REGISTER!" Reluctantly she opened it and I insisted she shows me the money. The bills were there in the order I described and with the fold on the five-dollar bill, just as I said.

She responded, "I'm calling the police." I walked out confused and angry and made my way back down to the street with visions of *horribillis* foreign jails swirling in my head. Thinking of prison food, I longed for the ship's increasingly desirable, never-ending buffet. Lucky for me the building was only one short block to the main street which led to the port.

As I scurried down the street, off to my left I saw a policeman. He was not in a 'looking for a fugitive' stance, leaning as he was against a building, arms folded across his chest with a bored look on his face and his eyes at half-mast.

My first reaction, when accosted, by the street store lady had been to give her the shirt and then thought, *No, why lose fifteen dollars and the shirt?* I reached the entrance of the port, thankful to be 'home free'. No one could get past security without proper I.D. beyond this point.

I then heard a siren. 'Oh, shit, now what?' As I walked to the ship, which was the furthest away, it appeared to be floating backward. As fast as I thought I was walking, as in a bad dream, I seemed to be walking in place in slow motion, not getting anywhere ... and it was HOT!

Feet!!! WALK!!! Finally, daring to turn around, I was relieved to see no one was following me. I finally relaxed. Perhaps the siren was not meant for me.

I made it back on board with a T-shirt to wear, a story to tell, and a warning to others to stay in the safety zones and, always, always, ALWAYS, get a receipt, and regardless, look before you leap, especially if you're on a boat!

FIFTY

Postscript

THELMA AND LOUISE

Stanley passed away. Gail and I made plans to go on a girls' trip, ala *Thelma and Louise*, but with an updated no cliff diving ending. I developed plantar fasciitis in my left foot. Plantar fasciitis is the inflammation of a thick band of tissues that runs across the bottom of one's foot and connects the heel bone to your toes. It causes a stabbing pain that advances and recedes like the waves on a beach.

That's about the last thing you want before going to Salt Lake City, Idaho, Wyoming, and the incredible Yellowstone National Park and Montana to do a little hiking. Ok, it's the second to last thing you want before going, being beaten only by traveling with your ex.

I hopped to Podiatrist #1 who promised to cure my heel by having me ingest his personally devised concoction of organic vitamins. The first ingredient in this assemblage was garlic, a plant that is wholly incompatible with my digestive system. My second visit to him ended with his hearty goodbye and good luck as I hobbled out of his office. That was my fault for even scheduling a follow-up with him.

After needing a second shot of Cortisone from Podiatrist #2, he suggested I try on a pair of sneakers that he had for sale. Unlike Cinderella, the sneaker didn't fit. He suggested that I have a mold made of my foot. I told him I had just bought Dr. Scholl's shoe inserts. He said his were better as he pulled them out from under his check-in counter...and his were cheaper. "How much do you pay for yours?" he asked.

"I don't know," I replied. I had bought a few things and didn't scrutinize the receipt. As I started to leave, he asked if I ever considered a Transcutaneous Electrical Nerve Stimulation or TENS treatment, and did I know what it is? I said, "Yes, it's the use of low-voltage electrical currents to treat pain."

He was visually impressed, and then said, "I have one that I can sell you for a good price." He followed me like a bad odor as I hobbled out to the elevator. I could hear him offering more pain-free items. Oh, what a relief it was when the elevator came, and his voice faded into nothingness as he continued hawking more miracle cures, as I began to descend deep into the elevator shaft as the words "magical elixir" echoed in the concrete trough.

"Hitchhiker's Guide"..., but not to the galaxy.

June 5th, 2021 was my first getaway after being in a pandemic lockdown for almost a year and a half. I am still praying for recovery from plantar fasciitis. Such a pretty name for such awful pain.

I contacted Southwest Airlines and requested a wheelchair for the two legs of my journey to Salt Lake City. They were very accommodating, and I was able to arrive at my hotel, Little America with a minimum of discomfort.

At 3: 30 a.m. on June 6th, still unable to put any weight on my left foot, Gail, a retired nurse, and Reiki Master, didn't like the swelling where Podiatrist #2 injected the second cortisone shot. She didn't like it?! It felt as though I was stepping on nails. She suggested I seek a medical opinion. No big deal. For the past ten years, I have had Emergency Assistance Plus travel insurance.

Now it's time for payback. I called the first of two phone numbers on my member's card. "We are having issues with our web site, and it will not be in service until Monday. Have a good day." Click.

The second, a toll-free number on the card answered and the woman suggested, "Find the closest hospital and make your way there." Click. So much for *'Travel safely knowing we have your back,* insurance'!

Gail called the front desk and asked where the closest urgent care or Emergency Room was and was told it was the Salt Lake Regional Hospital. She expressed the need for a cab and could someone come to our room with a wheelchair. After what seemed like, forever, there was a knock at the door. Hoping to see a wheelchair we were told the night clerk wanted to see what we needed.

"A wheelchair!"

"Oh, I'll be back" and he scurried away. He finally returned with the requested chair and after asking, said a cab had been called. He wheeled me to the main entrance to wait. After ten minutes I asked if the cab driver knew where to pick me up. "Oh yes," he assured me confidently. A few minutes later I glimpsed a cab pulling up in front of the sister hotel, the Grand America across the city street.

It was a little after 4 a.m. when I was dropped off at the ER. A young man sat at a desk behind a Covid proof shield. I sat in the chair at the counter filling out a brief form. He did not ask for any insurance info which I thought was strange.

A couple from Idaho came in and took seats in the waiting area, which was the size of a dentist's waiting room, and then left with a gentleman who came out from behind the ER doors. Now it was my turn.

After waiting for 'the room to be made up,' I was ushered in and hooked up to a blood pressure cuff and a splint-like oxygen monitor was taped to my finger. "What's wrong" the nurse asked? I gave her a brief description and started to take off my sneaker which she quickly instructed me to "Leave it on, it will keep it from swelling." Okay.

About ten minutes later Dr. Grayson introduced himself. He looked at my left foot asking some simple questions and announced, ala Arnold Schwarzenegger, "I'll be back." He returned shortly with one oxycontin and warned me that it was an opioid. He suggested other over-the-counter remedies, all of which I had been taking these past two months. I asked for padding to put in my left shoe to protect the heel. He said, which the nurse reiterated, a few minutes later, "Oh, we don't have anything like that."

He told me the side effects I could expect from the opioid and left. Only then, when someone walked by where I was still hooked up, did I suggest that if this drug worked, shouldn't I have a prescription? My question went unanswered although upon returning from wherever she went, the nurse did bring me a prescription, along with other papers which I did not read until days later. Lucky, I didn't need an amputation since the report showed my fasciitis was on my right foot.

I prevailed upon the nurse to fold gauze and make a pad to put in the arch of my shoe which she did and then, at my urging, instead, taped it to my left foot. I ripped off the Velcro blood pressure cuff but had trouble peeling off the finger monitor. With the assistance of another attendant, we were able to cut it off.

I went to the desk and asked the check-in man to call me a cab. It was now about 5 a.m. "Sure, he'll be here in about ten minutes," he responded. I took a seat in front of his shield to wait. About fifteen minutes later I asked when he thought the cab would show up. "In about five," he assured me. I asked him if he would like to see my insurance cards. With a smile, he said, "Sure."

After fifteen minutes I called the cab company and left a message. I then tried another cab company. "The number you have reached is no longer a working number." I called for a Lyft and saw that the closest one was going to be in fourteen minutes.

Deskman assured me, "The cab will be here any minute", so I sat down. The couple from Idaho had long gone and there we sat, just he and me. I waited a long time.

"You need to take a seat over there," he said. Since walking and standing were so painful, I questioned him. "We need this seat for emergencies."

"Oh fine, as soon as someone comes in, I will get up." Meanwhile, I kept asking about the cab.

"I gave him your phone number; he will call you as he gets closer." A few minutes later security came. Oh good, he's going to assist in getting me back to the hotel…wrong. It wasn't until much later that it dawned on me; the deskman called him to have me ousted from that seat to one in the even more desolate waiting area.

I explained my dilemma in not being able to walk and the delay in getting a ride. He suggested I take TRAX, a light rail system that was three blocks away, and once near the hotel, I would have to walk. I gave him that look that everyone's mother gives them when they do or say something really stupid.

The second choice was the city bus to the downtown mall and then transfer to the streetcar. I questioned his suggestion, saying the mall was not going to be open at 6 a.m. and I did not have a clue as to where I was. Lyft was still an option but now I was told the cab driver had been located and he would call when he got close.

Ten minutes later the security guy told me the city bus ran every five minutes, I said I would take the bus. He offered to push me, in the wheelchair, up the hill and across the street to the bus stop.

When we got there, he said, "The bus won't be here for at least another fifteen minutes." "What happened to every five minutes?" I heard myself squeak, now stoned by the Oxycontin. "I'm not going to wait, I don't even know where the bus is going. I'm going to hitchhike."

"Oh no, this is not a safe area," he said, as he took his leave, wheeling the empty chair down the hill, leaving me standing on one foot. Although we were on the side of the main road, at 6 a.m. on a Sunday in Salt Lake City, heavy traffic was not an issue. I tried flagging down cars and received smiles and waves back.

One car did pull over, a woman and her daughter. "Do you know how to get to the airport?" she inquired.

"No" I answered, "but" …and she drove off with her window sliding closed before I could finish asking her for a ride to the hotel. Her car had a New York license plate. I continued flagging down cars, continually receiving smiles and waves.

Eventually, a car passed by did a U-turn and pulled up in front of me. It was driven by a lovely young woman. Rolling down the passenger side window she asked, "Do you need help?"

I said, "Yes" falling gratefully into her car. I canceled the Lyft which showed it would be there in five minutes. Melissa was a scientist at the Children's Hospital and refused my thank you gratuity even when I suggested she pay it forward to a charity. I was back at the hotel close to 7 a.m.

I didn't know the room number. When we checked in hours before I didn't pay attention to it being that we were only going to be there one night.

While driving to the hotel I called and was told, "If you don't have the occupant's room number, we will not connect you to that person." I explained that I was sharing the room and had to plead with them to put me through to Gail who had left her cell phone on her night table. At home. In Jacksonville.

When I left, almost four hours earlier, she had gone back to sleep but was now awake. The oxycontin made me hungry and shaky. Gail met me in the hotel lobby and helped me hobble to the dining room that opened at 7 a.m.

And that, boys and girls, is the story of Day One, Thelma, and Louise hitting the Northwest for our first- girls-only road trip. I was so looking forward to Day 2.

~

My readers are the best critics! Please rate and / or review this book on your favorite book site or social media.

Also by Brenda Frank

Divorced After 56 Years - Why am I Sooo Happy?

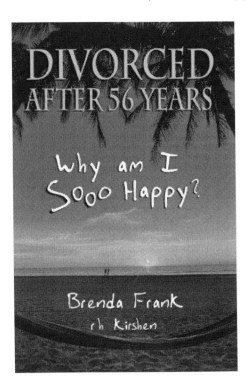

YOU'VE BEEN SERVED! How many people married for fifty-six years, and at the age of 75 have been served divorce papers? OK...but at a New Year's Eve Party? That humiliation, followed by the dissolution of my marriage, inspired me to write "Divorced After 56 Years, Why Am I Sooo Happy?"

The start of the new year was the birth of a new me. From what I learned, I earned the right to give advice with a smattering of zing, a touch of spice, and my own style of humor. And voila! this guide to the fun of being a party of one.

More than a divorce without remorse book, it's one that teaches, not preaches. Divorce is epidemic in America and like finding out you have an incurable disease that "will never happen to me", assume nothing. It can, and it did for me and for every person who reads this. My goal in writing this is to prevent the increasing number of divorcees and singles from making the mistakes I made while tripping and slipping to my own finish line.

Made in the USA
Columbia, SC
09 November 2021